# Guide to Green Fabrics™

Eco-friendly textiles for fashion and interior design

Kristene Smith

Published by:

Kristene Smith, Incorporated
Post Office Box 233553
Sacramento, California 95823

Library of Congress Control Number 2011909134

ISBN-13 9780975298398

First Edition

Table of Contents

## Acknowledgements

A special thanks to the following people for their contributions to this book: Ritu and Fanny for their content, research, and editing expertise; Roxanne for her excellent administrative support; our featured green designers and manufacturer; and the various teaching staff of Sacramento City College for their design insights, teaching styles, knowledge of textiles, and encouragement.

Appreciation also goes out to our production, printing, digital publishing and retail partners for their professionalism, direction, and kind support. Finally, special thanks to the Independent Book Publishers Association for their insights and timely advice.

Introduction

Eco-fabrics have certainly become a major source of curiosity as we all strive to green our planet a little more each day. This guide was designed to teach an understanding of the impact of green fibers and how they deepen our environmental awareness and commitment. It was written with the goal of expanding one's overall knowledge of textiles and to help empower fabric decisions in a fresh, new way. Because Guide to Green Fabrics™ is the most comprehensive resource of its kind on the market today, you'll enjoy every detailed chapter and learn many new things.

After reading about each type of fiber, you'll be able to decide which ones work best for you depending upon your design ideals and sustainability integration strategy.

Here's hoping you'll take full advantage of marrying your technical skills with today's green fibers to create exciting, new designs. Remember, it's the relationship you have *with* the fiber that will determine the outcome of your designs, so knowing the fiber's characteristics and how it performs in design is especially important to your project's success.

With that, congratulations on joining the green fiber brigade - those dedicated to a clean, green future on a global scale. Be inspired and find new ways to think like an environmentalist, yet with creative, cutting-edge, eco-style!

Warmest and Greenest Regards,

Kristene Smith

ant walking on abaca rope

Some therapeutic skin care products that are hand-crafted and sold as specialty items now contain abaca due to its high enzyme content. It's being added to cosmetics, soaps, and beauty creams throughout the world. Europe, the United States, and Japan are producers and marketers of such products, which reportedly have age defying properties that attract consumers worldwide.

"Creating a story about the fabric, how it's made, how it's dyed,
where it comes from, is beneficial since people don't always know."

Deborah Lindquist, Green Fashion Designer
Deborah Lindquist Eco Fashion Brand | deborahlindquist.com

# Guide to Green Fabrics

## Eco-friendly textiles for fashion and interior design

guidetogreenfabrics.com

# Abaca

## Overview

Abaca, technically referred to as *Musa textilis* of the family Musaceae, is known the world over by its more famous name, Manila hemp. A bast fiber, it is known as the strongest natural fiber and can be woven into a variety of airy textiles and interesting twines and braids. Even though it is known in the trade as hemp, it is very different from true hemp. True hemp is a soft fiber (a product of *Cannabis sativa*) whereas abaca is a hard fiber. It is obtained from the abaca plant, which belongs to the banana and plantain family. Most of the time these plants are mistaken for the banana plant itself (*Musa sapientum*). In contrast, the leaves of the abaca plant are narrow, pointed and upright, and taper more so than those of the banana.

These plants are indigenous to the Philippines, a reason why it has mistakenly been called Manila hemp. It has been cultivated there since the 1,500's and accounts for about 80% of the output of the fiber worldwide (about 50,000 tons per annum). Abaca plantations are found in the hot, humid upland areas and interior parts of the country, and are grown in regions like Bicol, Visayas and Mindanao. The rest of the bulk supply of abaca comes from Ecuador. Rich volcanic soil and tropical weather are ideal for the cultivation of these plants.

## Region

Having consistent, positive economic impact on the region, abaca has helped in the socio–economic advancement of the people of the Philippines. It is recognized as its flagship commodity, especially of the Eastern Visayas Region. Grown in 48 provinces, Catanduanes is abaca's top producer. The nine others are Leyte, Southern Leyte, Northern Samar, Davao Oriental, Surigao del Sur, Davao del Sur, Sulu, Sorsogon and Western Samar. The abaca plant has been introduced into different tropical regions including Indonesia, the Andaman Islands in India, the West Indies, and Central America. In Ecuador, abaca is grown on large estates, much in contrast to the small farm production common to the Philippines.

## Properties

The woven fabric is known as *Sinamay/Sinnamay*, a strong, open mesh fabric. New weaving methods have opened new vistas in design and its use is limited only by imagination. In fact, this fiber can be inter-twined with metallic threads to present a unique aesthetic. Abaca has superior tensile strength and excellent durability underwater. The fiber is actually stronger when wet. Because it's considered the strongest of all natural fibers, it makes a near perfect material for the production of pulp and paper, as it contains high levels of fiber. Abaca is resistant to salt water damage and was the preferred material for making marine cordage for ships before the advent of synthetic fibers. However, due to its strength, it can still be used in making hard wearing products, like cordage, for modern concerns. The beauty of its texture makes it a preferred medium in the production of hats and flower wrapping paper, and its fine qualities do not stop there. Abaca is also an anti-static, anti-microbial fiber that provides perfect ingredients for shampoos, soaps and detergents. It's reputed to have outstanding moisturizing and regenerative properties that assist conditions such as psoriasis and eczema through high levels of essential fatty acids retained in the fabric. Abaca is also known for its abundance of nutritious enzymes, and its high alpha cellulose qualities give it remarkable strength. Abaca is highly resistant to abrasions and has advanced fire resistant qualities. Naturally, it repels insects and rodents.

## Production

The abaca plant is a perennial plant that grows from short rootstocks. Numerous suckers grow from the rootstocks forming a cluster of stalks that are 10 to 25 feet high, and only abaca plants propagated from its rootstocks, not seeds, come true to type. It takes between 18 and 24 months for the appearance of the first stalk, then harvesting may begin. During harvesting, the trunk is cut down just above the roots. The length of the fiber varies from 3 feet to 9 feet and more, which is the length of the leaf stalk. The color of the fiber ranges from ivory to various shades of brown.

The fiber is obtained from the leaf stalk of a mature abaca plant generally containing about 25 fleshy, fiberless stalks that radiate from the central root system. It has long, broad, overlapping leaf stalks (*petioles*), 12 to 25 per stalk, and its crown bears large leaves that do not divide. Through the center, a flower stalk emerges upward and bears flowers followed by small, inedible, banana-like fruits filled with black seeds. Later, the seeds are pressed for oil and used in body care products. The leaf stalk is cut down to extract the fiber from its outer layer. In fact, all parts of the stalk from the outer dark layer to the innermost layers can be extracted, stripped, and processed. Lightweight, strong fabrics are made using the inner fibers, which generally are not spun.

The outer stalks are cut into thin sheaths and then into strips known as *tuxies*. The tuxies are pulled under a knife that is pressed against a block of wood by means of a bamboo sprig. The strips are then scraped either by hand or machine to remove the pulp, leaving behind the clean fiber. The cleaned fiber needs only to be hung-up to dry in the open air. After this stage, the fiber is ready to be graded and pressed into bales. For purposes of grading, the part of the stem from where it is obtained, the amount of serration on the stripping knives, and the degree of tension while holding the knife against the block are taken into account to determine the quality of the fiber. Promptness and care taken while drying also affect the grade and quality of the fiber. In Central America, a widely used mechanical method involves cutting the stalks and crushing and scraping them by machine, then drying the fibers mechanically.

## Environmental Concerns

This fiber is biodegradable and eco-friendly as abaca is mainly composed of cellulose, pectin and lignin. It is a sustainable material that replenishes itself through suckering. It is often used as a substitute for asbestos, which is carcinogenic and banned in many countries. Considering that abaca is processed by hand, the environmental impact is significantly lower than that of conventional fibers. An excellent crop rotator that leaves soil richer in nitrogen deposits, abaca requires no plowing, prevents soil erosion, and provides weed suppression. Promotion of *biodiversity* is possible considering that dependency on mass agricultural crop production is significantly reduced.

On average, it takes 20 years to harvest the most common trees, which are routinely used for paper production. Although abaca is not a seasonal plant it can be harvested for paper production in about 18 months, and has a greater yield per acre: about 4 (abaca) to 1 (trees). Therefore, as a world commodity we should look to abaca to service a wider variety of needs, including paper production, to reduce environmental impacts on a global level.

## Color/Dyeability

Being a natural fiber, abaca has similar dyeability potential as that of other natural fibers such as cotton, linen, and hemp - all cellulose or plant-based fibers. These fibers are best dyed under certain classes of dyes: fiber-reactive dyes, naphthol or azoic dyes, vat dyes, and direct dyes. Protein fibers will use other types of (acid) dyes that are better suited to their own properties, and still other kinds of dyes are used for synthetic fibers. Abaca happens to dye with excellence as it has no coating or dressing, so dye penetration is greatly enhanced. Abaca can be dyed into any color from earth tones to riotous tropical hues. It can withstand light colors all the way to neons and deep tones.

## End Uses

Abaca is ideal for both industrial and consumer applications. The traditional use of abaca was limited to making cordage and other allied products such as well drilling cables, fishing lines, fishing nets and power transmission ropes. In recent times it has become an important material for the manufacture of pulp and paper and is used for specialty carpets, vacuum cleaner bags, and table mats. Tea and coffee are packed in abaca bags (filters). Casing for sausages and other food products are made from abaca. The inner fibers are used to make tissue paper, newspaper, and packaging material. Truly, abaca is a multi-faceted product much in demand. Described as some of the most colorful people in the Philippines, the Bagobo wear beautiful clothing made of abaca. Due to the strength of the fiber, abaca fabric can be easily embroidered, beaded, and hand-painted with stunning results. The fabric beautifully maintains its shape, quality and natural luster. In India, it is used in the manufacture of denim. 40% of the Japanese yen is made from abaca, and in the Philippines, 20% abaca is used to produce 200, 500, and 1,000 peso bills.

Superior grades of abaca are used for fabrics, hats, slippers, rugs and various other items. Woven abaca, *Sinamay*, has little gossamer quality, but is quite transparent and very durable when compared to other natural fibers. Sinamay is used in the making of gift boxes, wall coverings, draperies, decorative accessories, footwear, tabletop accessories and many similar articles. It can be blended with softer fibers to produce more flexible textiles. The length, strength, and cellulose content of abaca makes it ideal for the manufacture of specialized paper for food packaging, electrolytic paper, cigarette filter paper and also some high quality writing paper. Abaca fibers also have several medical and industrial applications. It is used as an orthopedic material in joint and fracture healing implants. Abaca has also been proposed to be used as composite material to replace glass fiber in the manufacturing of cars, planes, and yachts. The stripping waste obtained during fiber processing is used as a growing medium for mushroom culture, as pulp for making hand-made paper, and as compost. Certain therapeutic skin care products that are hand-crafted and sold as specialty items now contain abaca due to its high enzyme content. It's being added to cosmetics, soaps, and beauty creams throughout the world. Europe, the United States, and Japan are producers and marketers of such products, which reportedly have age defying properties that attract consumers worldwide.

## Care

Abaca responds similarly to the care of other natural fibers. In all cases, it is best to try and remove stains promptly so they do not adhere to the fiber. It can withstand water better than other fibers, but because it is a hard fiber, wrinkling must be monitored in situations where abaca is a stand alone fiber, particularly for worn garments. Light detergent is best for use with abaca, while air drying and light ironing completes the care cycle.

## Abaca

Very abrasion resistant
Anti-microbial
Anti-static
100% biodegradable
Promotes biodiversity
Naturally colored from ivory to brown
Extremely durable, 3 times stronger than cotton
Dyes with excellence
Has advanced fire resistant qualities
Has natural luster
Has moisturizing properties
Remarkable physical strength
Naturally repels insects and rodents
Resistant to salt water damage
Prevents soil erosion
Sustainable, regenerates itself naturally
through suckering
Provides weed suppression

## Characteristics

bamboo rayon fabric

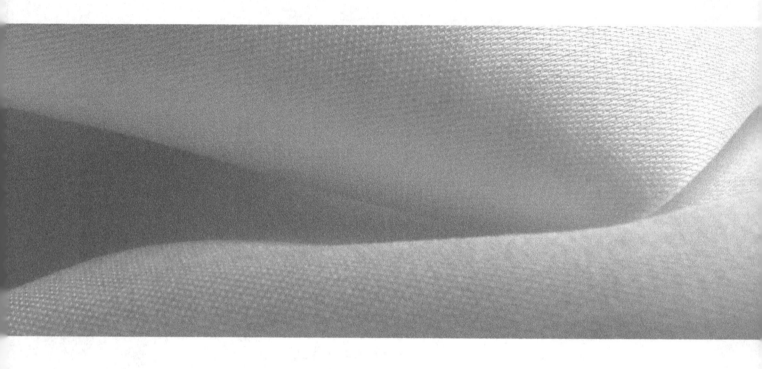

Bamboo is a green innovation which comes from a grass, not
a plant. Bamboo fiber is extracted and subsequently turned into
fabric that has the same rich look as lustrous silk, yet is durable
as cotton or wool. With this lush mixture of aesthetics, it combines
qualities which endear it to the green brigade.

"The world of fashion may be stylish, glamorous and exciting, but its impact on the environment is worsening day by day. From an environmental point of view, the clothes we wear and the textiles they are made from can cause a great deal of damage."

Namita Rautray, Eco-Manufacturer
Inovex Enterprises PVT. LTD. | inovexenterprises.com

# Guide to Green Fabrics™

## Eco-friendly textiles for fashion and interior design

guidetogreenfabrics.com

# Bamboo

## Overview

The word *green* previously solely referenced a family of colors reflecting a naturally bold and brilliant palette, soothing to all. Today, there is dual meaning of this word that is instantaneous and impacting on a global scale. Now, when we say *green* it refers to finding new ways to preserve nature, recycle, repurpose, and as consumers, participate in responsible ways when purchasing everyday products. As the eco-movement spreads, manufacturers are taking notice and finding ways of doing business that is good for the environment. In fact, innovations in green technology, sustainable product development, and enhanced recycling efforts are being realized globally.

The textiles and apparel industry, with its massive economic engine, touches every life. From clothes and bedding to car interiors and medical supplies, textiles are indeed woven into our collective fabric of life. New, green avenues are constantly being sought in this industry as well. Since everyday consumers generally do not have an understanding of textiles and their impact on the environment and the economy, textile manufacturers must take the lead in promoting these new innovations to attract like-minded consumers and their resources, and to educate customers on the benefits of going green.

One such innovation is bamboo (rayon, or viscose), which comes from a grass, not a plant. Bamboo fiber is extracted and subsequently turned into fabric that has the same rich look as lustrous silk, yet is durable as cotton or wool. With this lush mixture of aesthetics, it combines qualities which endear it to the eco-conscious. However, there are two distinct production methods detailed in this chapter, which will provide understanding of the controversy that bamboo may not be as green a fabric as was originally promoted.

## Region

Bamboo is found in almost all nations and hundreds of varieties of bamboo are cultivated. Most regions of Europe, Antarctica, and the Arctic do not have any native species of bamboo, although some countries have specifically started to cultivate the plant for its *environmentally-friendly* character. China is the largest producer of bamboo, which comes from a group of perennial evergreens in the true grass family *Poaceae*, sub-family Bambusoideae, tribe Bambuseae. One variety, *Moso* (*Phyllostachys pubescens*), can reach a mature height of 75 feet in just 45 to 60 days. We eat Moso bamboo found in many Asian dishes, but pandas love another variety. Used traditionally in hand-made paper production in Asia, there are over 1,200 species of bamboo globally. Bamboo is sustainable in both flood and drought conditions making it easily adaptable in almost any region. In China, organic bamboo is cultivated on over 7 million acres of family-owned farms, therefore posing no threat to tropical rain forests in other locales.

## Properties

One of its signature attractions is its breathability created by the micro-gaps and micro-holes that are present in the fiber. These tiny vents allow for increased air circulation, and its wick-like properties enhance its absorption qualities. Even at the height of summer a fashionista attired in garments made of bamboo can remain cool and chic knowing well that the garment will hold its appeal. This feature has earned the fiber a special nickname: air-conditioning dress.

Its anti-bacterial qualities make it ideal summer wear as it prevents formation of bacteria and fungi, which in turn create unpleasant odors. The anti-bacterial quality of the bamboo comes from the presence of a bio-agent called *bamboo kun*, which is bound tightly to the bamboo's cellulose molecular structure. This bacteriostasis agent arrests the growth and spread of odor causing bacteria giving bamboo fabric a feeling of freshness all day long. Even after 50 washes the fabric retains its anti-fungal, anti-bacterial nature, depending on the production process.

It is highly durable with a natural sheen and anti-static properties. A very unique quality of bamboo is its surface, which is round and smooth. This makes it non-abrasive and does not cause skin stimulation. Shrinkage and pilling do not pose problems for bamboo, and the woven fabric results in an airy, translucent and lustrous dream, with a result of being softer than the finest cotton. Just as bamboo kitchen cutting boards inhibit bacterial growth so does bamboo fabric, which makes it a top choice for towels, bedding, and baby diapers. In 2003, the China Industrial Testing Center tested 100% bamboo fabric and found it had a 99.8% bacterial kill rate. Most mothers would smile at those numbers just thinking about the protection of their darling babies.

With respect to its chameleon-like characteristics, bamboo viscose (rayon) is a leader in this category. It has the ability to mimic other fibers such as wool, silk, linen and rayon. It can be woven or knit into any type of fabric from denim to a slinky jersey. Other options include silky bamboo, bamboo canvas, double knit, terry cloth, shirting, and a variety of bamboo yarns for knitting, weaving, and crocheting. These fabrics generally resist wrinkling without the addition of formaldehyde (a carcinogen), which is added to polyester/cotton blended fabrics to give them those qualities. However, all wrinkling is not eliminated, especially for wovens. Bamboo has many of the qualities sought in performance and easy care fabrics without the drawbacks of synthetic material, and it has many of the fashionable qualities of silk, while being sturdy and vegan.

## Production

Bamboo is made from the pulp of the grass and is a cellulose fiber. Producing bamboo requires pulping the leaves and crushing the soft inner pith until the thin fibers separate. Certain patented technologies used for preparing it use a hydrolysis-alkalization process to extract fiber through a chemical process. This is the primary method of bamboo fiber production. Therefore, in most cases it is then soaked in a solution of 15-20% sodium hydroxide, which leads to the formation of alkali cellulose, which is crushed and dried. It is then made into a gel using carbon disulfide, which produces cellulose sodium xanthogenate, to which sodium hydroxide is added to create a rayon-like, viscose solution. This viscose, or bamboo rayon, cellulose is run through showerhead-like *spinneret* nozzles into containers of diluted sulfuric acid that reconverts it to bamboo fibers ready to be spun into yarns, which are sometimes bleached. Depending on the size of the yarns, bamboo can be extremely thin. However, it has great tenacity and elasticity. It quite resembles cotton at this stage and handles much like cotton yarns. From there, bamboo can be woven or knitted into beautiful, lustrous fabric, which resembles silk depending on the weave. Alternately, there is a mechanical process similar to hemp or flax production which involves crushing the stalks while natural enzymes work to further break down the pulp. The fibers are then combed out and prepared for *spinning*. The result of the mechanically produced bamboo is a much harder and stiffer fabric, which is not widely marketable for garment production, so it is much less in demand. Both processes were developed in China, the world's leading producer of bamboo.

The dilemma presented here involves understanding the chemical process associated with developing bamboo fabric. The chemical production process mirrors the process used to develop rayon, or viscose. Although the original source of the pulp may come from organic bamboo, the process is still chemically intensive. Through this process, some of the benefits of the original bamboo are lost, such as the anti-microbial and biodegradable properties. These chemicals are also harmful to the environment via air and water emissions. Therefore, the U.S. Federal Trade Commission has demanded that manufacturers of "bamboo" fabric provide a more accurate labeling to consumers based upon the process of production, rather than the source of the cellulose. With this, consumers will begin to see bamboo labeled as "viscose bamboo" or "bamboo rayon," and these are the reasons therein. However, mechanically processed bamboo can indeed be called "bamboo" or "organic bamboo." Consumers should check the manufacturer's certifications, such as Oeko-Tex, should there be concerns about its eco-authenticity.

## Environmental Concerns

For a fabric to be truly environmentally friendly, its methods of cultivation and impact on the surroundings are important considerations. Bamboo scores high on this parameter as it is a sustainable, fast growing plant without pesticides, fertilizers, defoliants, or herbicides. It enhances the quality of the soil in which it's grown and cleans up the atmosphere of greenhouse gases via natural absorption of carbon dioxide. A renewable resource, it not only absorbs up to 60% more carbon dioxide from the environs, but also enriches it by releasing large amounts of oxygen, about 35% more than what is produced by an equivalent stand of trees. Soil quality is improved due to bamboo's extensive root system, which holds soil together and prevents erosion, plus watershed retention is realized. Bamboo cultivation needs minimum human and mechanical input, thus eliminating the need for fossil fuel-powered tractors for sowing and harvesting. Due to its biodegradability, (mechanically produced bamboo, that is) bamboo fabric decomposes into the soil by sunlight and micro-organisms without releasing any harmful gases, such as methane, a harmful by-product of decomposing waste found in dumps and landfills, into the atmosphere.

## Color/Dyeability

Bamboo absorbs dyes more efficiently than modal, viscose, or cotton, thus eliminating the need for intensive dyeing. The fabric does not have to be put through the process of *mercerization* as the luster obtained after dyeing is in itself extremely attractive.

## End Uses

Because of its chameleon-like qualities, bamboo finds application in numerous items of apparel and furnishing. Its odor-free character makes it well adapted for making garments, under-garments, t-shirts and socks. Its excellent wicking ability makes it ideal to be worn close to the skin. Its high absorption makes it ideal for manufacturing sanitary items and surgical bandages as well as bathrobes, towels, and bath floor mats. Bamboo's anti-bacterial quality (via mechanical production) also makes it widely applicable in the medical supply industry for textile items. Being ultraviolet-proof, it is used in making curtains, slip covers, wall coverings, and for purposes of outdoor decoration.

## Care

Bamboo fiber and its final products require very little maintenance. Washing instructions are simple as it can be washed on the gentle cycle and tumble or line dried like that of other natural fibers. It is similar to cotton in ironing (medium-high heat) and has very little shrinkage. Bamboo has been a staple of Asian societies for centuries and has more than 1,000 documented uses internationally. It's considered an easy care fabric because it can look and drape like silk, but is more practical because consumers can use a machine wash on the gentle cycle and dry bamboo in the dryer or on the clothesline.

## Bamboo

Abrasion resistant, non-irritating
300% more absorbent than cotton
Does not require agricultural tending,
tractors or planting devices
Anti-bacterial
Biodegradable (mechanical production only)
Breathable, thermal regulating, cool
Deodorizes, keeps you odor free and smelling fresh
Excellent draping qualities, much like silk
Takes well to dyes
More elastic than cotton
Enriches the soil
Hypoallergenic
Insulating, keeps you cool in summer and warm in winter
Naturally lustrous, similar to silk
Grows without need for pesticides or fertilizers
Avoids pilling and shrinkage
Resilient and durable
Extremely soft, silky hand, feels like cashmere
Naturally strong fiber
Sustainable resource, grows plentifully
Naturally UV resistant
Excellent moisture wicking abilities

## Characteristics

Defined as *the diamond of clothing*, a new and spectacularly eco-driven luxury fiber called Cervelt™ has emerged onto the fashion scene. Poised to remain a rare fiber, it is obtained from the red deer of New Zealand, which boasts the world's largest population of this prized creature.

"Producing using organics or earth friendly fabrics is more expensive. There is a growing demand for these items, but it will take time for the pricing to evolve. You can do incredible things with natural fabric, they are fantastic to work with."

Beth Doane, Green Fashion Designer
RainTees | raintees.com

# Guide to Green Fabrics™

Eco-friendly textiles for fashion and interior design

guidetogreenfabrics.com

Cervelt™

Defined as the *diamond of clothing*, a new and spectacularly eco-driven luxury fiber called Cervelt™ has emerged onto the fashion scene. Poised to remain a rare fiber, it is obtained from the red deer of New Zealand, which boasts the world's largest population of this prized creature.

Extraordinarily well cared for, these deer are provided with spacious, beautiful grounds to roam naturally and stress-free. They drink unpolluted river water, breathe pure air, and nestle amongst unmatched, tranquil scenery.

Because only a small amount of fiber can be taken from one of the deer, about 20 grams maximum, it remains rare. This fiber is soft and smooth, lying close to the deer's skin, and is protected by coarse outer hairs. Each hair measures approximately 13 microns in diameter, making it finer than the finest cashmere. It would take the inner hairs of at least 14 red deer to produce one finished sweater, and 40 deer for a single overcoat. Therefore, it is understood that production limits will always apply making it a rare and expensive luxury fiber. As an added benefit, the fibers are also manufactured in environmentally-friendly ways.

To solidify its position in the market, Cervelt™ presents the following facts, it is: 200 times rarer than gold, 3,000 times rarer than cashmere, and nearly 2 ½ times rarer than diamonds. These natural production limits have caused the manufacturer, Douglas Creek™, owned by Richard Keddell and the McGhee family, to be especially selective with product development partners. Select Italian partners, including Lanificio Fratelli Bacci™ from Florence, Italy, bring to life Cervelt™ fabrics, fashions for men and women, accessories, knitwear, and furnishings. Only a few, highly qualified brands are involved with product distribution.

Cervelt™ fashions are pill-free due to the fiber's coil-like qualities, which add lightness, softness, and elasticity. It's an absorbent fiber providing comfort in cold and warm climates alike. Cervelt™ is very stable and resilient and does not easily crease. It stays very warm irrespective of the fabric's thickness or thinness. A full range of hues are available from light to dark with excellent colorfastness.

"Coconut fiber has a high lignin content and thus a low cellulose content, as a result of which it is resilient, strong, abrasive and highly durable. The remarkable lightness of the fibers is due to the cavities arising from the dried out sieve cells."

Namita Rautray, Eco-Manufacturer
Inovex Enterprises PVT. LTD. | inovexenterprises.com

# Guide to Green Fabrics™

## Eco-friendly textiles for fashion and interior design

guidetogreenfabrics.com

Coir

## Overview

One of the oldest fibers known to man, coir is a product of the coconut, one of the earth's first trees. The coconut tree (*Cocos Nucifera L*), a palm tree species, has many interesting myths about its appearance as well as its great benefits. A typical tree will produce an average of 75 coconuts per year, and the fruit is always in various stages of maturity. Therefore, it delivers a year-round harvest. In Indian mythology the tree is considered as a kalpa-vriksha, or the "wish-fulfilling tree," and in modern interpretation it can be considered so because it fulfills the economic and material aspirations of those who cultivate it. These trees can grow up to an amazing 100 feet tall.

The word 'coir' was derived from the Malayalam word 'kayar,' which came from the Tamil word 'kaya-ru.' It means "to be twisted," as in rope or thread. Centuries ago, Indian navigators who sailed the seas to Java, China, Malaya, and the Gulf of Arabia used coir for their ships' cables. During a visit to the Port of Hormuz on the Persian Gulf in the 13th century, Marco Polo learned that master Arab seamen sewed their ships together with coconut fiber without using any nails. He also found that the Chinese boasted a 500-year history of using coir. The coconut tree from which the fiber is obtained is well known for being a plant whose each and every part finds usage. Coir fiber is obtained from the part of the fruit between the husk (*exocarp*) and the outer shell of the coconut. The husk has a smooth, waterproof outer skin (*epicarp*) and fibrous zone called *mesocarp*, which is embedded in non-fibrous connective tissue as fibro-vascular bundles. This is referred to as *coir pith*. Coir has been used for millennia by the people of Asia. The earliest mention of it being extensively used as ship cables, fenders, and for rigging, came from 11th century Arab chroniclers. However, there's an even earlier mention dating back to 60 AD when a Greek sailor noted that an East African village was sewing together its boats with coconut fibers. With the advent of colonialism, it was soon traveling to various parts of the globe to be used for ropes and mats. There are records from the latter half of the 19th century, which attest that there was in fact a coir industry in the United Kingdom. In fact, the very well known carpet firm, Treloar and Sons, used coir in fabric production.

## Region

Coir production is concentrated mainly in the developing nations and India, especially its southern state Kerala, a narrow strip of land wedged between the Western Ghats on the east and the Arabian Sea on the west. India accounts for more than 60% of the total worldwide production. Sri Lanka, a neighboring island of India, accounts for another 36% of the fiber produced, while other locales include Indonesia, Vietnam, Mexico, and some Caribbean nations. Combined, Sri Lanka and India produce 90% of the 250,000 metric tons of coir produced annually. In India, over 80% of those employed in the coir industry are women.

## Properties

Coir contains narrow, hollow cells with thick cellulose walls that take on a hard, yellow layer with the deposition of *lignin* in the walls. It is an exceptionally tough natural fiber being capable of absorbing water up to twice its weight without any expansion in volume. It is made up of cells or threads that are 10 to 20 mm in diameter and less than 1.3 mm in length, with the average coir fiber being 10 to 30 cm long. Its major constituents are lignin and *cellulose*, the 45% lignin content providing its strength and stiffness.

Coir is brown colored when made from fully ripened coconuts, while the white fibers are harvested at the unripe stage. The brown fiber is extremely thick with enhanced strength making it adaptable for use in mats, ropes, and sacking. The unripe, white fibers have a very smooth look and fine texture, but lose out on strength. The yarn made from white fibers is fashioned into mats. The differences in characteristics between the two types of fibers are due to different extraction methods as well as the use of both mature and immature husks. Coir's unique color has earned it the nickname "gold fiber." It is also known in other countries as "cocos fiber."

## Production

After the fruit has been removed, the fiber is extracted from the coconut. This is generally done by hand. The fruit is driven through a spike secured to the ground, which splits it in a process called *de-husking*. The speed at which man achieves this task is very fast, and seasoned huskers are known to have de-husked up to 2,000 coconuts a day. With new technology making its way into these highly traditional and conservative practices, machines have been employed and do the work of humans in less than an hour.

The extracted fibers are then soaked in shallow pools of slow running (fresh) water to swell and soften them. This process of *wet-milling* separates the long bristle fibers from the shorter under-fibers. The shorter mattress fibers are sifted in order to remove any dirt, and then are usually dried in the sun and packed into bales. Some are allowed to maintain a degree of moisture so that they can retain their elasticity for twisted fiber products. The longer fibers go through a similar process of washing and drying, but these may also go through another process of straightening meant to remove the shorter fibers amongst them so as to create a more consistent batch of fibers.

The process for making the white fiber is slightly different and involves *retting*, during which the immature husks are soaked in fresh and seawater for a period of about 10 months. This long period of soaking in water allows nature to take over the process, and micro-organisms attack the plant tissues allowing the fibers to be loosened from the decomposed husk. Researchers discovered that by adding 10 anaerobic bacteria to the water (those that live without oxygen) in a broth-like solution, it hastened decomposition, yet kept the fiber composed. The soaked husk is then beaten by hand with a wooden mallet and the long fibers are dried, cleaned, and spun into beautiful, strong yarns, often using a spinning wheel called a *charka*. As of late, machinery has largely enhanced the spinning process to achieve increased production value.

It should also be noted that the retting process generates a significant amount of water pollution due to the release of several major organic pollutants such as pectin, tannin, and pectosan, as well as a variety of bacteria including salmonella. However, there is research underway to find treatment options for these waters.

There are a variety of beautiful yarns made from coir: Aratory, Vycomme, Anjengo, etc., each one being different based upon the thickness, luster, twist, texture, quality and length. The yarns are spun on *ratts*, which are both mechanized and traditional. Presently, global fiber production is at around 350,000 metric tons. Despite its renewability and plethora of applications and uses, even in India and Sri Lanka this fine resource is underutilized.

While coir is a biodegradable and renewable resource, it takes about 20 years to completely decompose, and this meant that until the 1980's, extremely large quantities of unused fiber would just sit around in huge piles in India and Sri Lanka. Toward the end of the 1980's, scientists managed to create various technological and chemical processes, which allowed for coir to be made into mulching, soil treatment and a hydroponic growth medium.

Coir fiber gives out a by-product, coir pith, which forms almost two-thirds of the coconut pulp, which was in earlier times given up as useless. Newer technologies and research methods have found many uses for this voluminous by-product, and it gives rich dividends to producers and eliminates stress on the environment. Coir pith retains water and is highly compressible making it ideal as a soil substitute, mulch, and conditioner. It is also known as *coir dust*.

Some of the greatest environmental benefits of coir are seen in its use as a *geotextile*. It is used for covering the ground while landscaping as a means of preventing soil erosion. Because the texture of coir is somewhat hairy, it offers excellent cling-ability to seeds and soil. The fiber has very high air and water permeability, allowing enough sunlight to pass through, which gives young plants and saplings adequate nutrition while at the same time keeping them safe from rough winds. Typically, shorter brown yarns that have abbreviated retting periods are used as geotextiles. Recently, coir pith has become a highly absorbent product meant to mitigate the effects of oil spills.

Erosion from the sea eats away the shoreline, which can be controlled by placing coir fabrics along the shore. Its natural resistance to salt water and biodegradability makes it ideal for slope stabilization and bioengineering. These fabrics boast an average 4-year lifespan for these purposes, and then begin biodegrading into the soil.

Coconut husk also contains fine materials and fiber that make-up an environmentally important commercial by-product called *coco peat*. A homogenous material, coco peat contains millions of capillary micro-sponges that have an extremely high ability to absorb and retain water. Being renewable, it is an acceptable substitute to mined peat moss, which now has much slower production as a result, and is a bonus to halting extraction from environmentally compromised swamps. Thus, coco peat is affordably and effectively used in the horticulture industry in a variety of regions.

## Color/Dyeability

Coir's best dyeing method is the mechanized method whereby the dyeing liquid is run across fibers that have been arranged symmetrically. Excess water is drained out by *hydro-extractors* after which the fiber is passed through the endless conveyor drier for quick, uniform drying. In order to dye fibers in pastel shades, the fiber is first bleached and then dyed. Colors tend to show better absorption when the fibers have been wetted prior to the dying process. Green husks yield the most suitable, retted fibers for dyeing and bleaching. Through conventional methods, coir would be cooked in a vat of dyeing ingredients over an open fire, occasionally stirred, and then left to dry out in the shade. While that would suffice for home and personal use in a local village, industrial and commercial products require the efficiency and constant quality offered by the mechanized system.

## End Uses

Coir finds its most plentiful use in the production of household items like doormats, mattresses, ropes and twines, and is also used for brushes. With the introduction of *needle-felting*, a process in which fibers are matted together, coir blocks are fabricated for use in stuffing mattresses. Individuals with allergies may need to watch their exposure to coir, a known allergen to those with sensitivities. The automobile industry uses a form of coir on which latex has been sprayed that helps in binding the fibers more effectively. This rubberized coir is used for padding in automobiles, is a natural fire-retardant, and is not easily combustible. For gardening, coir pots are fashioned as natural, biodegradable receptors for tomato and other plants across the world.

## Care

Coir products are popular in fabricating outdoor items, which are prone to the vagaries of the weather. Being immune to dampness and moisture, it retains its inherent properties even in adverse weather conditions. Caring for coir products is an easy task, as slight tapping loosens the accumulated dirt and dust. It does not need dry cleaning and color spoilage is minimal.

## Coir

Very abrasion resistant
Airy and porous, has excellent aeration abilities
100% biodegradable, returns to the earth in closed loop fashion
Needs no chemical treatment, pesticides or herbicides
Raw material compatibility is superior, can be planted with other plants
Expandable, can hold up to 5 times its weight in water
Flame-retardant
Less flexible than cotton or flax, due to lower cellulose content
Provides great insulation against both temperature and sound
Mildew resistant even for stored fabric
100% organic
Naturally renewable, viewed as an important agricultural resource
Repels snails and other garden pests
One of the few natural fibers resistant to salt water damage
Resists mold and rot
Excellent color retention ability
Has extremely high water retention properties
Outstanding capacity for wetting and re-wetting

Characteristics

"I think people are aware, but not always spending money on green goods because they prefer cheap, throwaway merchandise these days. It's really disturbing and more prevalent than ever. Creating awareness has to be somewhat entertaining to capture anyone's attention, and it has to make sense in people's lives. Since you're talking about the fashion industry and not just the fabrics, that has to be included too."

Deborah Lindquist, Green Fashion Designer
Deborah Lindquist Eco Fashion Brand | deborahlindquist.com

# Guide to Green Fabrics™

## Eco-friendly textiles for fashion and interior design

guidetogreenfabrics.com

Corn Husk

## Overview

It is the endeavor of agricultural environmentalists to utilize to the maximum the crops they grow and to keep waste products to a minimum. Keeping this in mind, various experiments were carried out to find ways of intonating corn husks and leaves into productive uses since they constitute an enormous amount of by-product after the harvesting of corn. For example, after the feed corn has been harvested by shucking the ears of corn from the stalks, the husk is discharged by the harvesting machine onto the ground where it remains along with the leaves to be ploughed back into the field before the next crop is sown. As a solution to this wasteful process, the husks, blowing out of a combine, are now utilized as fiber to bring not only greater economic gains for farmers, but also as aid to the environment. Corn husks are readily available in voluminous amounts making them extremely economically attractive for fiber production.

## Region

Corn is grown in almost all parts of the world with the U.S. being one of its largest producers, and the availability of raw material for producing corn husk fiber is never in doubt. The application of these husks and leaves for the purpose of creating fabric is dependent more on the will of humans using it rather than dependence on availability of raw material, which is a prime concern when developing other fibers.

## Properties

Scientists at the Institute of Agriculture and Natural Resources at the University of Nebraska have converted corn husks into high quality textiles. The naturally off-white color of the fiber is very attractive and shows better comfort than synthetic fibers. It has good dyeing potential too. Corn husk fibers exhibit properties that mimic those of cotton and linen in strength, while the length of the fiber is more like that of cotton. It is softer and more flexible than both cotton and linen with greater load bearing capacity, imparting strength to the fabric.

## Production

The method of extracting fiber from corn husks is accomplished through a process that involves, as a first step, drying out the husks and leaves to a moisture free state. After the moisture has been allowed to escape, the corn husks and leaves are soaked in an *alkaline bath*, consisting of 5% to 25% sodium hydroxide, for a period of about 1 to 5 days at room temperature. This immersion in the alkaline bath loosens the fiber from the vegetable matter while at the same time imparts a degree of strength to the fiber. The fiber is then rinsed to remove all traces of the *caustic solution* and any other impurities. Afterward, excess moisture is removed so the fiber can be dried. The fiber is combed on a woolen carding machine to straighten and arrange it in parallel rows, then it is formed into 2 bundles. These bundles are allowed to pass through a solution of *ethylene glycol* that lubricates the tow and aids in the manufacture of twine, one of the leading products made from discarded corn husks. The use of corn husks to make twine was prompted by the poor economics of growing and producing sisal fiber and twine in the U.S., as sisal-based twine was the preferred material for binding bales of straw. The climatic conditions and immense labor requirements rendered sisal cultivation non-viable in the U.S. leading to the discovery of creating fiber from corn husks.

## Environmental Concerns

The impact on the environment has been positive considering that the utilization of waste product to create a material of great utility is considered noteworthy within the environmental community. It is indeed a renewable resource that is readily available worldwide. Not only this, it also curbs consumption and thus transportation of great volumes of other material, and this significantly lowers carbon emission levels. Production of the fiber is extremely simple, and without excess mechanical input, makes it not only a green option, but also an economically viable one. In addition, corn cultivation calls for far fewer fertilizers and pesticides when compared to traditional textile fibers like cotton.

The application of corn husk serves not only human needs, but also aids the environment by removing pressure that is brought upon it when growing materials that have only one purpose, that is, for producing fibers only. Making it a multi-purpose crop, corn satisfies the dietary needs as well as fiber concerns of ever increasing populations, making it one of the greenest fibers on earth.

## Color/Dyeability

The dyeability of corn husk is similar to cotton, and when blended with it, the resulting fabric shows good application in garment manufacture.

## End Uses

Twine is the most notable product made from corn husk. Other products include craft items, art supplies, utility baskets, and fashion tote bags.

## Care

Corn husk is sometimes blended with other fibers. It should be washed according to the instructions given on the garment.

## Corn Husk

### Characteristics

Natural, off-white color
Offers better comfort than synthetic fibers
Has good dyeing potential
Greater load bearing capacity than cotton
Has long natural fibers, like cotton
Renewable resource
Has similar qualities to cotton and linen
Softer and more flexible than cotton and linen
Strong and durable

"Maintaining ecological balance is a major issue confronting the corporate world today. The damage done to the environment has already crossed the threshold and reached alarming limits. Non-replenishable natural resources are getting depleted at a rapid pace. Generation of waste, including biodegradable pollutants, is increasing enormously. All these negative developments have forced mankind to think more seriously about conserving the environment."

Namita Rautray, Eco-Manufacturer
Inovex Enterprises PVT. LTD. | inovexenterprises.com

# Guide to Green Fabrics

### Eco-friendly textiles for fashion and interior design

guidetogreenfabrics.com

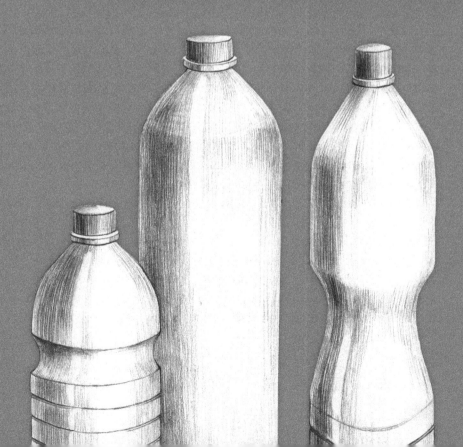

Eco-Fi®

## Overview

Should someone mention that he/she were wearing clothes made of plastic, our first reaction would be of incredulous disbelief and a complete negation of such a possibility. However, what seems impossible to the layperson is now reality through the pioneering efforts of scientists at U.S.-based Wellman, Inc.™. This innovative enterprise decided to do something about the millions of petroleum-based plastic bottles littering the planet and choking the earth, taking us slowly toward certain environmental disaster. While the advantages of using petroleum-based plastics has allowed for technological and economic progress, it comes with an obvious downside, that being the seemingly infinite use of oil. Because petroleum products are not *biodegradable*, the *refuse* ends up creating veritable mountains of empty plastic bottles in landfills, which are eventually burned, releasing toxic pollutants into the atmosphere.

Over 40 billion plastic bottles are produced in the U.S. each year, and it becomes apparent what a huge environmental problem this is considering that less than 30% of these bottles are recycled. The pioneering work of Wellman, Inc.™ delivers an innovative solution responsible for lowering impact on landfills and the environment. That solution is EcoSpun®, or EcoFi®, as it has been recently rebranded; an artificial fiber made from 100% recycled plastic bottles. Currently, its estimated production could very well utilize 3 billion bottles annually, thus canceling-out the need for 500,000 barrels of oil while eliminating 400,000 tons of harmful air pollutants. The new name EcoFi® was developed by Foss Manufacturing, Inc.™, Wellman, Inc.'s™ exclusive manufacturer.

## Region

Being a fiber that is man-made, EcoFi® can be created worldwide in factories equipped with the right machinery and access to raw material. In this case, discarded plastic bottles and other equivalent plastic packaging material.

## Properties

This fiber offers its best performance when blended with other fibers. It is most commonly blended with wool, cotton, or Tencel™. The resulting fabrics are generally lightweight, warm, and soft with amazing strength, and very comfortable to wear. It has some of the advantages not found in natural fibers, the most important being extreme colorfastness and lack of shrinkage. Recycled polyester is another variation of EcoFi® and is a common, interchangeable term in today's fashion industry. It is made from both post consumer and post-industrial P&T (*Polyethylene Terephthalate (PET)*) waste, while the latter is made exclusively from P&T bottles. The raw materials used for making either are abundantly available, and by using discarded materials, the production of these fibers aids in protecting the environment. At the same time, utilizing waste materials that burden the ecosystem is a bonus and these innovations have gained quite a bit of traction in the market.

Some of the advantages of using these fibers comes from their synthetic nature, which discourages growth of bacteria and microbes leading to a mold and mildew free fabric even when wet. Both have anti-wrinkle properties and do not exhibit shrinkage. Recycled polyester also has high strength and durability. Due to the significant length of the yarn, protruding ends are eliminated leading to lint-free and pill-free fabrics. The fabric is extremely low maintenance and can be machine washed and dried, and requires no ironing.

## Production

The process used to create fabric from plastic bottles begins with sourcing the bottles from local recycling facilities that package and transport it to the processing plant. The sorting process begins with the removal of labels and caps then the bottles are sorted by color. The bottles are then sterilized before being crushed and chopped into tiny flakes, which find their way into large vats ready to be melted. The process of melting these flakes is carried out with simultaneous stirring until the flakes have been turned into a rich, thick liquid ready to be extruded through a spinneret, which looks much like a shower head. Once extruded through the spinneret, the liquid is transformed into strands of silky polyester. Stretching the fibers allows for strands to be created in various thicknesses, lengths, and strengths. The fibers are then crimped and cut into shorter pieces and readied for shipping. The task of turning these strands into fabric is completed by knitting and weaving.

## Environmental Concerns

EcoFi® so impressed the United Nations, one of the foremost crusaders of environmental protection, that they awarded Wellman, Inc.™ with the first Fashion Industry Award for Environmental Excellence. This prestigious award turned the spotlight on this revolutionary fabric and soon designers, apparel makers, the furnishing industry, and accessory makers were making a beeline for the fabric whose versatility and functionality opened new vistas in design. All those who doubt the quality of the fabric can rest assured that the plastic used has already passed the stringent controls of the U.S. Food and Drug Administration, making it one of the top-notch eco-fibers available.

EcoFi® is a wholly green fabric, in that it responsibly uses a resource which has become a bone of contention between environmentalists and manufacturers. Giving it new shape and using it in a way that even the most ingenious green crusader might not have imagined has reshaped its destiny. The positive impacts of this fabric on the environment are significant considering the innovative recycling process of truckloads of discarded plastic bottles being turned into yards of beautiful fabric. The wider adoption of EcoFi® will help counter environmental problems in new and unique ways. Take into consideration that approximately 10 large bottles equals almost a pound of fiber, and that twenty-five 2-liter bottles can become a medium sized fleece pullover. Indeed, the environmental potential for this fiber is very high. In its manufacture, EcoFi® uses minimal amounts of water, one of our most precious and limited natural resources. The use of harmful pesticides and fertilizers is totally eliminated as it is created from discarded synthetic materials.

## Color/Dyeability

Similar to the raw material from which it originates, EcoFi® can be colored in as many hues as needed so as to compliment other fibers woven with it. Like traditional polyester, the liquid solution is already colored prior to yarn processing, therefore allowing it to become extremely *colorfast*.

## End Uses

This fabric features very good insulation properties, and for this reason, it is most commonly used in creating sports clothing, especially those for outdoor activities. Its capacity to retain heat makes it perfect for the manufacture of thermal undergarments, sweaters, and socks.

It is also used to create knapsacks and beddings for use in outdoor sporting activities because it is extremely lightweight. EcoFi® velvet is one of the most sensuous and silky fabrics made from this fiber, and finds a wide range of application in home furnishings and accessories.

When used to make fleece garments, it delivers a soft and colorfast product, which is nearly functionally and chemically identical to fleeces made from non-recycled material. EcoFi® can also be fashioned into carpets, wall coverings, automobile interiors, as filling material for cushions, and craft felt.

## Care

This fiber is relatively easy to care for since the manufacturing process itself manages attendant difficulties found with natural fibers. However, being machine washable and dryable, care requirements will partly depend upon other fibers that it may be combined with, so knowing characteristics of the blend is important. Garments created from this fabric can be laundered by following manufacturers' washing instructions.

## Eco-Fi

Blends easily with other fibers
Extremely colorfast
Comfortable especially when
blended with natural fibers
Durable, stable fabric
Requires no ironing
Lightweight, ideal for sportswear
Extremely low maintenance
Maintains petroleum base through recycling
Mold and mildew-free fabric
Length of yarns allows for pill-free fabrics
Shrink resistant
Soft, drapable, silky appearance
Strong, has exceptional strength
Wrinkle resistant, smooth finish

## Characteristics

# Designer Spotlight

## Sarah Barnard

Working out of her Los Angeles based studio, Sarah Barnard works on interior design projects large and small, from sprawling corporate headquarters to cozy beach front cottages. With a contemporary approach that employs traditional vocabulary, she defines her range of style as "innovative yet time-honored." Sarah Barnard Design undertakes residential interior design projects, commercial spaces and even single rooms. She works with clients on space planning, color counseling, kitchen and bath remodeling, historic preservation, and all aspects of green design and healthy living: organic, non-toxic, sustainable and fair trade materials, energy and resource conservation, air and water purification, natural furnishings, fabrics and more. Some of the green fabrics used in her designs include wool, cotton, bamboo, silk and linen. "Home and occupant health can be improved by having textiles that are organically grown and milled without chemicals. These textiles make for better, cleaner indoor air quality, potentially reducing allergies. There is also the satisfaction of supporting sustainable farming," states Sarah. She employs an overall eco-conscious way of designing, procuring, and doing business. Her company manufactures locally and in small quantities working with responsible companies only. Her vendors must be committed to recycling since her offices recycle and her employees strive to make eco-friendly choices in their everyday lives. Raised in a family of historic preservationists and conservationists, she was naturally attracted to sustainable design and feels it's her responsibility to design safe, non-toxic spaces for her clients. She states, "It has become increasingly common that homeowners express sensitivity to toxic materials used in their homes and actually suffer from symptoms like headaches, nausea and even depression. Because we have observed such positive changes in health life by purging these chemical products, we have made it our goal to do so for whosoever is willing." With organic linen as her favorite fabric, she enjoys working with other natural fabrics and sometimes uses recycled, non-toxic options that are still better for the environment. She acknowledges the design industry's movement toward going green and considers the process to be a life-long one with people continually recommitting to a sustainable lifestyle. Sarah's top five suggestions for creating awareness of the importance of green fabrics: educating people to create awareness, public understanding and recognition of the importance of making green choices, promotion and advertising of green fabrics, sharing eco-conscious information within families, and choosing a green lifestyle.

Sarah Barnard Design | sarahbarnarddesign.blogspot.com

Lone Pine Pictures                                                                                          Brad Nicol

Today, as homes are being built or renovated with green products, eco-leather furniture offers warmth and a cozy feel. Leather sofas are associated with class and sophistication, being not only comfortable, but the aging process imbues them with a certain patina that emits warmth and a sense of luxurious living.

# Guide to Green Fabrics™

### Eco-friendly textiles for fashion and interior design

guidetogreenfabrics.com

# Eco-Leather

## Overview

From the Roman soldier of classical times to the magnificently draped divas of our time, leather combines both style and functionality, as its fascinating appeal continues to endure. Surely, it will capture the affection of generations to come. Interestingly, leather-making may have been a serendipitous happenstance, probably discovered when animal skin lying in wet forests became tanned with chemicals that were released during the natural decaying process, as well as through interaction with forest vegetation. Through trial and error, man subsequently found various ways to soften and preserve raw animal skin and turn it into durable leather. Indeed, even prehistoric man realized that a material that kept animals adequately covered against the elements would help keep him safe too.

Natural processing of raw animal skin into leather continued to be practiced until the discovery and introduction of chemicals like lime and sulphuric acid. Unfortunately, the use of chemicals made large-scale production of leather a series of processes that caused damage to the environment. The use of chrome, formaldehyde, sodium sulphide, glutaraldenhyde and other metals put water and air at risk through seepage and toxic fumes. Today, conventional tanning methods using chrome are being replaced with healthy and environmentally friendly *vegetable tanning* methods. Hence, eco-leather, which as the name suggests, is as friendly to the environment as it was centuries ago when it was first discovered. For the sake of a greener planet, production of eco-leather has once again drawn attention to the benefits of these natural and abundantly available processing methods.

The term eco-leather has no specific definition, but is used to denote leather, which is made by employing earth friendly techniques using *sustainable* products, especially vegetable products and *natural waxes*. For leather to be considered as eco-friendly it has to be produced using *clean technology*. The process of manufacturing must be controlled, and the use of restricted substances ought to be managed effectively so as to cause minimum harm to the environment.

## Region

Hides used to make eco-leather come mostly from South America, as the cows that are reared in this region are *organic* in nature. These cows are not certified as organic, but since they graze freely on huge expanses of pasture that grow naturally, their organic label is pre-determined. Most eco-leather producers use animals that are raised organically, while other manufacturers use surplus hunted animal skin. Tanning may take place locally or in other regions, such as the United States.

## Properties

Today, many consumers base their purchasing decisions on factors such as ethical involvement in product development, high quality, and environmental friendliness. To satisfy the growing demand for credible eco-products, the EcoSure® mark has been established, which helps consumers identify eco-leather from the ordinary. Eco-leather has unique characteristics. Marks of its natural origin are visible in a healed scar, or *growth marks*, which are a result of damage caused by barbed wire or horns of cattle. With the passage of time it develops a *patina* that adds to its natural beauty giving it distinct characteristics. Indication of the age of the animal from which the hide is taken can also be deciphered by growth marks and veins.

The texture of leather varies and is relative to the pore structure of the hair on the skin. These pores are the reason for the varying grain pattern. In untextured leather, sometimes the open pores are visible. The grain variation also leads to uneven dye penetration and thereby it provides attractive variations. Eco-leather has high tensile strength and it is resistant to tear. This fiber does not puncture easily. It has good insulation and contains a great deal of air, which is a poor conductor of heat. The fibers hold large quantities of water vapor, which enables it to absorb perspiration. Eco-leather has *thermostatic* properties, meaning it is warm in winter and cool in summer. The fiber is inherently resistant to flame and heat. It has both plastic and elastic properties and can be molded easily. It is also resistant to fungi such as mildew.

## Production

Conventional tanning techniques involve a complex process where use of heavy toxic chemicals contaminate water and emit toxic fumes, but eco-leather dramatically reduces these occurrences. The prerequisite toward the production of eco-leather is the use of efficient processes that reduce water consumption, energy use, and *carbon emissions*. The production of eco-leather uses *natural tanning* methods, which utilizes organic materials such as extracts from bark and vegetables, rather than traditional tanning chemicals. Chemicals necessary for tanning eco-leather are produced from farm bred Mimosa trees, thereby eliminating the use of toxic heavy metals. In addition, the use of harmful chemicals can be reduced by reversing the order of the tanning process, as discovered by scientists at the Central Leather Research Institute in Chennai, India. Changes are also incorporated in the post tanning process, and by following simple procedures, the release of harmful chemicals is cut down by 82% and energy efficiency is raised by 40%.

## Environmental Concerns

The environmental friendliness of leather is dependent upon two important parameters: the method of tanning it, and secondly, the inputs used in manufacturing. Eco-leather manufacturers around the world have realized the need to reduce their *carbon footprint* and have therefore started using alternative, renewable sources of energy. This aspect of processing helps in cutting down carbon emissions. In addition, eco-leather can be disposed of in an environmentally safe manner. Its own characteristics help in the process of degradation and recycling. The growing popularity of eco-leather has also helped to reduce leather waste. This fiber is an earth friendly alternative to conventional leather, and its harmony with nature, in relation to raw material, manufacture, and disposal, is undisputed.

## Color/Dyeability

Eco-leather is dyed using naturally occurring vegetable dyes available in a wide range of popular colors. It can also be custom dyed to specification. Natural wax is used to provide the final finishing. Eco-leather is also available as printed fabric. These leathers can be dyed in bright colors too.

## End Uses

Eco-leather was used by early man for the purposes of clothing and shelter, but today we find it being widely used in varied industries with virtually unlimited applications including furniture upholstery, fashion accessories, and as fabric.

Today, as homes are being built or renovated with green products, eco-leather furniture offers warmth and a cozy feel. Leather sofas are associated with class and sophistication, being not only comfortable, but the aging process imbues them with a certain patina that emits warmth and a sense of luxurious living. Increased public awareness on issues regarding the environment has brought about a shift in the mindset of people, and though people have not given up this classy, traditional material, they are now opting for eco-leather sofas and other pieces. Typically, these sofas are very durable and have no hairline scars or blisters.

As it has become more accessible, this fabric has gained popularity in the past two decades. Consumers find its softness and durability very appealing. It can also be printed, therefore providing a great range of choice for the consumer. For the style conscious, fashion accessories made from leather never go out of style. Be it everyday wear or high fashion, leather accessories add rugged charm and sophistication. Eco-leather provides the fashion industry with more options in creative freedom at minimal environmental harm.

## Care

Eco-leather upholstery is very easy to clean. Care should be taken to remove spills by immediately cleaning them with distilled water and an absorbent cloth. Because the fiber does not take very well to detergent, cleaning agents, ammonia, oil, and saddle soap, these products are best avoided. Instead, to remove tough stains, commercially available leather care products can be used. To ensure that such products are safe, it's advisable to use them first on a non-visible area, and if there is no adverse result, then the leather care product can be applied to the affected area. Keeping such leather products away from sunlight is also important to maintain its general well being and long lasting appeal.

## E-Leather

E-leather, a recycled product for modern times, is made using leather that is obtained from discarded leather. In earlier times, wet blue-waste leather from tanneries was used for landfill, but now they are processed to make e-leather. This leather is extremely soft and of very high quality, making it not only consumer friendly, but also an environmentally friendly, recycled product.

There are several advantageous, eco-conscious process applications used to produce e-leather. These include the use of high-pressure water jets to clean the leather and tangle it, and it is chemical-free. Plus, there is an absence of oil-based adhesives used in conventional bonding, thus reducing our carbon footprint. Clean technology provides the muscle to "loop" the process by regenerating emissions from solvents via *thermal oxidation*, and this regenerated fuel acts as clean energy in the manufacturing process. Indeed, many stringent regulations are met during these steps. As a bonus, non-toxic water recycling remains a foremost activity used in production, offering a total *closed-loop* process, which is clean and green.

E-leather is a renewable source that is produced by recycling clothing, automotive materials, and other landfill-bound leather waste. E-leather has found use in various sectors such as footwear, automotive, aviation, marine, transport, commercial upholstery and leather goods.

## Organic Leather

Organically raised animals that graze freely, roam at their leisure, and generally live under stress-free conditions produce hides that generally classify as organic. Should their hides be tanned organically as well, then the resultant leather would classify as organic leather. Both conditions must be present for this classification to apply. Because this type of leather is not yet very common, the expense for organic leather is out of reach for some. Products made from this leather include bags, belts, and furniture. As organic methods become more commonplace while logistical production issues align, market demands will shift providing accessibility to a wider range of consumers.

## Eco-Leather

Anti-bacterial, mildew resistant
100% biodegradable
Breathable, allows for air circulation
Extremely durable, practically lasts a lifetime
Susceptible to fading in direct sunlight
Fire retardant
Has naturally healed scar or growth marks
Hypoallergenic
Has excellent insulation properties,
keeps you warm
Pliable and flexible, can be easily shaped
Resistant to tearing
Scuff resistant
Smooth, soft touch and feel
High tensile strength
Has thermostatic properties
Free of toxic chemicals

## Characteristics

naturally colored hemp fabric

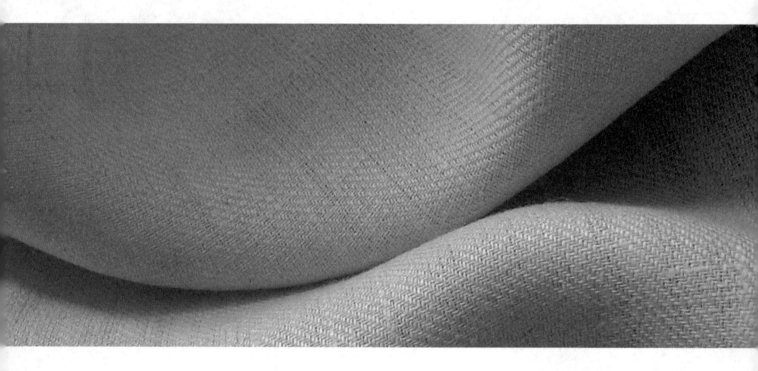

Many hemp fashion and interior products are designed without any
additional coloring. This adds appeal to hemp's standing as a green fiber,
much to the delight of those seeking purely natural resources for design.

"I have faith in the next generation. They are the building blocks of our future and they are more aware, less self-orientated, and more proactive than mine. As they take their places in industry, then I believe it will change."

Isobel Davies, Green Fashion Designer
Izzy Lane Ltd | izzylane.com

# Guide to Green Fabrics™

## Eco-friendly textiles for fashion and interior design

guidetogreenfabrics.com

Hemp

## Overview

Cultivated from plants of the *Cannabis genus*, hemp is one of the most environmentally friendly fibers, but due to its association with marijuana the positive qualities of the plant have been somewhat pushed to the background. At one time, negative publicity and a relentless drive against marijuana plants reduced this once thriving plant into a rarely grown crop, especially in the United States. Countries like China have been cultivating hemp and producing hemp textiles for the last 6,000 years, and its multifarious applications along with easy cultivation practices endear it to farmers and fabric producers alike. It originated in Central Asia and eventually found its way to India and Europe to be used as food, medicine, and for fabric production. An early domesticated plant, hemp is one of the fastest growing biomasses and is capable of creating 25 tons of dry matter per *hectare* per year.

In America, the decline in hemp cultivation has been attributed to William Randolph Hearst, the publishing magnate whose economic interest in the forest industry directly clashed with hemp cultivation. Using his newspapers, he launched an attack on the hemp industry equating it with marijuana use and soon hemp cultivation dropped dramatically. The reach of his powerful media empire made people oblivious to the fact that even Washington and Jefferson, the founding fathers of the United States, cultivated hemp on their farms. In fact, the Declaration of Independence was first drafted on paper made from hemp while Benjamin Franklin's paper mill made paper only from hemp.

The strength, durability, and low cost of hemp made it the fabric of choice for army uniforms, and Napoleon's soldiers were outfitted in hemp uniforms. During World War II, even the U.S. Army used hemp for uniforms, ropes, and canvas. It was used in ships to secure sails, as it is highly resistant to saltwater rot and thus ideal for sea-going vessels.

## Region

Hemp is widely cultivated on almost all continents, but Russia remains its largest producer. In Europe, France is one of the chief producers of hemp, though considerable areas in the U.K. and Germany are also known for hemp cultivation. Austria, Australia, Canada, China, Spain, Japan, Philippines, North Korea, Hungary, Romania, Poland, and Italy are some of the other countries that grow hemp. It can grow in a range of soils, but tends to prefer those that produce high yields of corn. Ideally, the soil would be well drained, non-acidic, and rich in nitrogen. Mild, humid climates with an average rainfall of at least 25 to 30 inches (64-76 cm) per year suit it best.

## Properties

Hemp is a bast fiber, extracted from the soft part of the plant found just outside the woody inners of the stalk. The fibers are very long, ranging from 3 feet to 15 feet depending upon the length of the stalk. Depending on the processing method used, the extracted fiber can be grey, black, green, creamy white, or brown in color. The fiber is extremely strong and durable and has excellent absorption properties while at the same time repels ultraviolet rays. The texture of hemp is very close to that of linen.

## Production

Hemp production calls for large inputs of labor for the process of harvesting, drying, and retting. The plants are ready to be harvested for high quality fiber when they start shedding their pollen, usually in mid-August in a temperate climate. Hemp is ready to be harvested 70 to 90 days after seeding, and specialized cutting equipment is required. Modern, mechanical harvesting methods offer specially adapted cutter-binders, or a more simple cutting process may be employed. The fibers are then laid in swathes for several days, which allows for air to circulate amongst the fibers. Once the crop is cut the stalks go through the retting process. After retting, during which the plant is soaked in water, the stems are bundled up into small rolls and passed through a series of rollers to get rid of any leftover wood and stem. Modern retting processes can vary from using enzymes and chemicals in order to hasten the process, to using ultrasound technology. Steam machines may also be used for fiber separation. This more modern process is referred to as *thermo-mechanical pulping*. Once the bast fiber is separated from the woody core of the stalk, it has to be cleaned and *carded* to the desired core content and fineness. The resulting hemp yarn can be used to weave or knit a variety of fabrics and textile products. The pulp meant for making paper can then be used for special applications such as industrial filters, tea bags, cigarette papers, and currency notes.

## Environmental Concerns

The renewed interest in hemp cultivation comes from increased environmental consciousness among people the world over. Due to its deep tap root system, minimal water requirements enable the plant to reach the subsoil and extract water for its use. The plant reaches heights of 5 meters on average at a very fast rate and is characterized by lush, dense foliage which prevents weed incursions, in turn eliminating the need for spraying *herbicides*. In comparison to cotton, hemp requires little or no pesticide application. All these qualities give it a green halo. In fact, an acre of hemp gives as much pulp for paper as 4.1 acres of trees, which makes it ideal for paper production with lower impact on the environment. There is very little chemical input in the pulping process and the natural brightness of the fiber reduces chlorine bleach application. Hemp has good chemical compatibility with hydrogen peroxide, a bleaching agent, which brings down negative environmental impact.

## Color/Dyeability

From black/brown and beige to tan and sage, naturally-colored hemp offers a pleasing rainbow - naturally soothing in organic-looking shades. Many hemp fashion and interior products are designed without any additional coloring. This adds appeal to hemp's standing as a green fiber, much to the delight of those seeking purely natural resources for design. Otherwise, the fibers can be easily dyed in pretty much any color conceived. The crucial steps are the process and the ingredients used for dyeing. In order for hemp to be considered organic, the dyes used and the processes involved must be equally environmentally conscious.

It's important to note that even though one might think that natural dyes should be exclusive for green fibers, many use more energy and employ harsher chemicals than lab produced dyes. Disposal methods must also be considered for their negative environmental impacts including irreversible harm to rivers and streams. Alternately, low impact and fiber-reactive dyes are water-soluble and don't contain heavy metals. Hemp takes to these types of dyes with ease.

The hemp plant also allows for fiber extraction from its woody core, which makes up about 70 to 80% of the plant. Rich in lignin and cellulose, they are ideal for making paper as well as biomass fuel, rayon, biodegradable plastics, food additives, and cellophane. Man has utilized hemp for centuries to make cordage and ropes for securing objects, canvas for purposes of storage, and textiles for garment production. The paper industry makes archival grade paper from the plant, while in the construction industry it is used as a strengthener in conjunction with concrete, and at the same time reduces shrinkage and cracking. In the apparel industry, hemp is used to make accessories, jeans, pants, bags, and cargo pants, among other items. For interior design purposes, retailers offer hemp shower curtains, light drapes, table cloths, slipcovers, and bed covers. A heavier version is also used as cork-board covering.

Hemp also produces fruit from which seeds are extracted, pressed for oil, and applied to a range of products. Oil-based paints, cooking oil, plastics and moisturizing oil are common hemp-related products. Domesticated birds also enjoy hemp seeds in their seed-mix, and fishermen have been using hempseed as bait for decades.

By-products of harvested hemp are also useful in other applications. The core fiber can be used to make paper, mulch, horse bedding, litter, and construction materials. Hemp dust, created during the production process, is pressed into pellets and used for fuel, and small chips from the core are used as a high nutrient soil additive.

## Care

Apart from its cultivation, manufacture, and dyeing processes, which are highly environmentally friendly, hemp fabric is easy to take care of both in matters of storage as well as cleaning. Being naturally moth-proof, there is no need to take extra precautions in storing items made of hemp. It is dirt resistant and any dirt which accumulates can be easily washed off in a machine without much concern for temperatures or settings, as hemp handles hot and cold variations quite easily.

In case of discoloration of white hemp, the color can be restored by ordinary washing and sun drying, which restores the fabric's fresh hue. Bleaching should be avoided as it weakens the surface of the fabric. Being highly water absorbent, hemp dries very fast. While still slightly damp, hemp fabric can be easily stretched into shape and ironed on hot settings.

## Hemp

Excellent absorption properties
Naturally colored from creamy
white to black
Easy to dye
Grows in a range of soils
Naturally moth-proof
Grows without pesticides or herbicides
Highly resistant to saltwater rot
Strong, extremely durable fiber
Texture is similar to linen
Repels ultraviolet rays

## Characteristics

Hand painted details on bamboo rayon napkins by Kristene Smith

sisal craft flower

Henequen withstands extreme wear and tear and is anti-static.
This fiber is relatively dust and grime free. Depending on the
surrounding air humidity level, this fiber will either absorb or
release water, thus causing it to expand or contract accordingly.

"In families, greener choices may be made when knowledge is shared and everyone encourages others to go green. If all these steps are combined, awareness of the importance of sustainability and green fabrics will spread."

Sarah Barnard, Green Interior Designer
Sarah Barnard Design | sarahbarnarddesign.blogspot.com

# Guide to Green Fabrics™

Eco-friendly textiles for fashion and interior design

guidetogreenfabrics.com

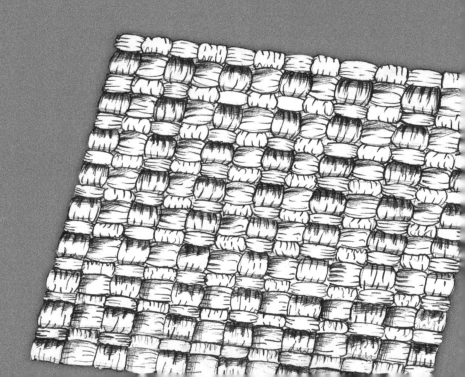

Henequen/ Sisal

## Overview

Henequen has almost always been synonymous with the Yucatan region of Mexico and the economy of Yucatan owes much to this strong, sturdy, resilient fiber. The wealth derived from henequen created some of the Yucatan's most magnificent haciendas and made this Mexican state one of the most prosperous in the country. It is one of the oldest fibers used by man, and the life of the Maya and Inca people was dependent on it to a great extent. They used it to make not only ropes, cables, and lassos, but also fashioned curtains and other accessories for their homes. They made hammocks for their outdoors and thick fabrics for personal wear.

The fiber obtained from this plant continued to be used by succeeding generations of Mexicans for a multitude of purposes. The Spaniards who conquered Mexico called it by its Mayan appellation *tsootquij*, which soon became synonymous with sisal, and the two terms are used interchangeably by some to this day. The Spanish conquistadors used it to make cables for their ships and bags for storing grain. But that was the glorious past when the fiber was used to make burlap bags, which met more than 90% of worldwide demand. Like some other agricultural industries this too became a victim of the industrial revolution and scientific advances, and very soon the twines and ropes obtained from it were replaced by synthetic ones. As if this were not enough, the Mexican revolution occurred and henequen/sisal became one of the casualties of the general unrest and economic uncertainty. The biggest impetus to the henequen industry came when the *reaper* was invented by American Cyrus McCormick. This machine was used to cut standing grain that was then tied into bales using thin wire, which was often ingested by cows piercing their stomachs and making them sick. When nylon ropes were used to tie the bales they too were ingested by the cows leading to sickness. It was then that henequen ropes were used to tie bales of cattle feed, and being a natural fiber, even upon ingestion by the animals, was easily digested and did not cause harm. Ever since, this has been one of henequen's most important applications. In addition, its ability to survive saltwater ravages found favor in the shipping industry before the onslaught of steel ropes and cables.

## Region

Mexico is the pre-eminent producer of henequen and this fiber is synonymous with the country, although the cultivation of the plant is nowadays carried on in several parts of the world. Some of the countries engaged in producing the fiber in significant quantities are Brazil, Tanzania, Philippines, Madagascar, Venezuela, and Florida in the United States. Being a very tough plant, it survives in even the most hostile of environments and while several other crops cannot survive a drought, henequen remains unaffected by lack of rainfall. This makes it especially popular as a cash crop in developing countries where irrigation systems are relatively less developed and cultivators have to depend on rainfall for water.

## Properties

Henequen withstands extreme wear and tear and is anti-static. The fiber is relatively dust and grime free. Depending on the surrounding air humidity level, this fiber will either absorb or release water thus causing it to expand or contract accordingly. When it expands, it is a highly absorbent fiber. Henequen fabric can also serve as a fire retardant after it has been treated with borax. It has also shown great promise in a series of scientific studies, which explored methods of incorporating the fibers into various types of *polymers* for purposes of features enhancements.

When treated with specific compounds, the tensile strength of henequen increased by 268%, its elongation at break by 110%, and its elasticity by 300%. While this was meant to study its possible applications in construction building materials, it is interesting to note the potential of these fibers.

## Production

The fibers are obtained from the long, spiny leaves of the agave plant (*Agave fourcroydes*), which grows to a height of 2 to 4 feet with a width of 4 to 8 inches. The leaves are very thick, ranging from 1 to 4 inches. It is an extremely slow-growing plant and reaches full maturity after 4 years or when the stem comes to a diameter of about 8 inches. It is only then that the leaves can be harvested. Over a period of one year not more than 25 leaves can be harvested, and during its lifespan the plant yields about 185 leaves. Afterward, it loses its use as a fiber yielding crop.

The process of extracting fiber from the leaves involves crushing and pulping the leaves. In its initial stages the fiber is coarse, but the pulping turns it soft and pliable almost comparable to silk. First, the harvested leaves are run through a large wheel that splits them thus exposing the gut, which contains the raw, yellow fibers, which are then laid out to be dried. The dried fibers are then bundled and put into machines that shed the fibers, while at the same time untangling the matted mass. These thick fibers are then put into another separator to create fine strands, which are finally sorted out according to their thickness and identified for use in various products. Finally, the individual strands are wound by varying thicknesses.

## Environmental Concerns

In spite of its low output, what makes this plant attractive for cultivation in these environmentally conscious times is its high disease resistance, which eliminates the use of pesticides. Being the tough, sturdy plant that it is, henequen is known to have survived even fires. It prevents soil degradation by being an effective trap for moisture and is a good blocker of *soil erosion*. Despite some apparent short-comings, especially in the large amount of waste biomass produced as a result of fiber extraction, what works in favor of this plant is its use as cordage, woven products, and pharmaceutical items, and that offsets the loss. On the upside, these large amounts of biomass are also being used as bio-fuel and as animal feed, especially for beef cattle. Henequen finds its place on the list of environmentally friendly fibers not so much on account of its cultivating practices or methods of production, but rather as a fiber that is a more effective substitute for synthetic fibers and materials for certain products. Due to chemical intensity, production of synthetic fibers negatively impacts the environment, and as a viable alternative to these, it makes this fiber environmentally preferable in many respects. Another factor that works in henequen's favor is that it provides livelihood for vast populations in developing countries while at the same time meets the needs of developed nations in ways that are in tune with healthy, sustainable practices.

## Color/Dyeability

Although flexible for a variety of uses, henequen fiber is used mostly to create binding and packaging products, and therefore does not require any coloring. However, henequen fibers are very accepting of a variety of dyes, especially acidic ones. In the interest of maintaining the environmental friendliness of the fabric and for creating traditional handicrafts, natural dyes are the preferred choice.

These dyes are sourced from plant barks, leaves, flowers, and seeds. In the Yucatán region, the local flora and fauna provide the best colors, and innovative handicraft artisans sometimes toss in pieces of metal that transforms the color, giving a vivid palette from which the artisans of the region create beautiful wall hangings. Being extremely easy to dye, henequen simply requires an open fire and a large aluminum pot when used in conjunction with natural dyeing methods, such as bark or other plants. Once the dye has been released into the hot water, widely available compounds such as alum or bicarbonate soda may be added in order to fix the color or intensify it. The fibers are then incorporated into the hot, now colored, water and stirred to desired result. Fabrics may then be rinsed of excess dye and hung out to dry. Obviously, this method is meant for personal use or for very small batches of fibers. Mechanization has reached all aspects of life and industry, and when it comes to industrial quantities there are faster and more effective methods in place. Some of the most common colors in which henequen fabric is found are brown, orange, yellow, beige, green, grey and black.

## End Uses

As a sustainable fiber, henequen can be used to make long-lasting shopping bags, geotextiles, pulp for paper industries, construction materials, sturdy furniture items, as padding in mattresses and sofas, as well as in the automobile industry. As a reinforcement material, it is used in composite plastic manufacture, especially in auto components. Brake pads use henequen as a substitute for asbestos. Its use as agricultural twine is the most important application of the fiber while as a geotextile it meets a great demand. The lightness of the fabric makes it preferred summer wear. However, the fibers are so strong that the limited production is generally diverted away from fabric making and is instead purposed as cordage, twines, matting, and rugs.

## Care

Henequen/sisal, like most naturally rough fibers, tends to develop dark spots on the surface when used for rugs and mats, and while it does not attract dust, it can be easily stained. To remove stains, dabbing with a wet cloth is recommended instead of washing it completely, and for more daily maintenance, vacuuming will suffice. Due to its ability to absorb or release water depending on the environmental humidity, it is not recommended for use in areas prone to a lot of spills, rain, or snow.

## Henequen/ Sisal

Highly absorbent in a humid environment
Has anti-static properties
Generally dust-free
Takes especially well to natural dyes
Extracts water in dry climates
Becomes fire retardant when treated with borax
Hard, sturdy, stable hand
Naturally long fibers harvested every 4 years
Grows without the need for pesticides or herbicides
Naturally renewable and sustainable
Saltwater resistant
Strong and durable

## Characteristics

One of the finest man made fabrics not sourced from synthetic materials bears the name Ingeo, which means "ingredients from the earth." As the name suggests, raw material for the fiber is procured from natural sources such as plant starches, particularly corn.

"When you see endangered species disappearing forever because of pesticides and toxins that we are creating, it's heartbreaking. Like so many things it's a matter of education. People can't be inspired to change something they don't know anything about."

Beth Doane, Green Fashion Designer
RainTees | raintees.com

# Guide to Green Fabrics™

Eco-friendly textiles for fashion and interior design

guidetogreenfabrics.com

Ingeo

## Overview

One of the finest man made fabrics not sourced from synthetic materials bears the name Ingeo, which means "ingredients from the earth." As the name suggests, the raw material for the fiber is procured from natural sources such as plant starches, particularly corn. These materials are biodegradable and can be *recycled*, burned, and turned into compost with hardly any adverse effect upon the environment.

Like all synthetics, the fibers come equipped with good strength, high tensile properties, and good resistance to wear and tear. Ingeo has the added advantage of being less susceptible to ultraviolet rays, one of the main causes of radiation brought about by ozone layer depletion. South Korea, Taiwan, and Mainland China are the leading producers of Ingeo.

## Properties

Being a cellulosic fiber, its characteristics are akin to silk, wool, and cotton in touch, feel and texture while requiring very little maintenance. It is fire-resistant, odor-free, and has good *wicking* properties. Ingeo is also more resistant to ultraviolet light than most other synthetic fibers.

## Production

Ingeo is the result of chemical processing involving procedures of basic fermentation, distillation, and subsequent polymerization. Naturally occurring starches found in plants such as corn are broken down into sugar, which is made into a *biopolymer* (PLA). The resin is then used to create plastic goods via injection molding, and thermoformed into packaging. It is also extruded for film and textile applications.

## Environmental Concerns

Cargill Dow LLC™, a company behind the production of this fiber, set out to create a product that would balance nature, technology, and human aspirations, and ultimately make a positive difference to the world. While many people blame scientific advancement as one of the chief causes for the radical, negative changes in the environment, some technological advances through prudent application help to sustain the environment. As evidenced, one of these is the use of *biotechnology* in using plant resources to create synthetic fibers.

What sets it apart from other synthetic fibers is that it is produced from a *renewable resource*. Unlike nylon, which uses petroleum as a raw material and whose supply is limited and not biodegradable, Ingeo is sustainable as a green product for many uses.

## Color/Dyeability

Ingeo is a highly versatile fiber. While it comes from a natural and renewable source, it is very unlike cellulose or protein fibers when it comes to its chemical makeup. It is much closer chemically to polyester and this means that it is also dyed using the same processes and ingredients.

## End Uses

Due to its synthetic nature, Ingeo fibers are used widely in home furnishings, yet the resultant fabrics look quite natural. Carpets made of Ingeo are the preferred choice for designers and homemakers who are looking for sturdiness coupled with an ability to resist soiling and dirt accumulation. Common, effective applications of Ingeo can be found in shopping bags. Ingeo is a natural choice for furnishings including bedcovers, drapes, and paneling. In addition, personal care products call for a high level of softness to touch and a tendency toward being abrasion-free, and Ingeo fulfills these beautifully.

## Care

Garments and home accessories made from Ingeo show an extremely easy maintenance routine. Products can be washed at home using standard cleaning procedures. It has quick drying properties and retains its shape remarkably well without the added task of ironing.

## Ingeo

Abrasion-free fabric
Biodegradable, fibers are easily burned
Has characteristics of silk, wool, and cotton
Dyes extremely well, like polyester
Has fire resistant characteristics
Acts as an odor barrier
Tends to be quick drying
Easily recycled
Good resistance to wear and tear
Has soft texture
High tensile strength
Has ultraviolet resistant qualities
Offers good wicking properties

## Characteristics

jute produce bags

Jute is a very important geo-textile and is used to make containers
that are used in the planting of young trees. Its biodegradability
allows for direct planting of the container into the soil and over
time jute degrades naturally.

"Humans interact with the environment constantly. These interactions affect quality of life, years of healthy life lived, and health disparities. Environmental health consists of preventing or controlling disease, injury, and disability related to interactions between people and their environment."

Namita Rautray, Eco-Manufacturer
Inovex Enterprises PVT. LTD. | inovexenterprises.com

# Guide to Green Fabrics™

Eco-friendly textiles for fashion and interior design

guidetogreenfabrics.com

Jute

## Overview

Jute, "the golden fiber," looks all set to capture our hearts and homes alike as the new darling of innovative designers. Its versatility and green qualities have sparked the imagination of that band of designers and accessory makers who have made a pact to wed design with sustainability.

From seed to the expired fiber, there is no part of the plant that can be cast aside as waste material. Jute gives only main products and extremely useful by-products, none of which are wasted. The uses of Jute range from the common rope to designer jute silk that graces the homes of the rich and famous, and of course, the green brigade. Its subtle earthiness makes it the perfect complement to designer homes that are now created around the back-to-nature theme. From drapes to upholstery, from rugs to throws and floor mats to place mats, Jute fulfills all the accessorizing needs of modern homes in keeping with best environmental practices.

In times past, the jute fields of pre-independence India filled the coffers of England and sparked a revival of interest in this plant. Going forward, it promises to bring increased prosperity to those farmers whose livelihood depends upon it. Jute is a predominantly Southeast Asian crop and is cultivated in India, Bangladesh, China, and Thailand.

## Properties

Elementary jute fibers are short in length measuring between 0.7 to 6 mm while the longer fibers, 3 to 4 cm long, are the result of the short fibers attaching themselves to each other through lignin. Only about 39.5% of the plant contains fiber while 48% is wood, and the remaining 12.5% is comprised of leaves. Jute is a complex mix of cellulose, hemicelluloses, and lignin. The *hemicelluloses* make it sensitive to alkali while the cellulose makes it sensitive to acid, rendering the chemical processing of the fiber extremely delicate. Jute has good insulation against sound and light as well as being anti-static and a low thermal conductor.

## Production

4 to 6 months after sowing, the plant reaches its full maturity and is ready to be harvested. The harvesting process is followed by retting. This process separates the *phloem*, which contains the useful fiber, from the *xylem*, which is the woody core.

Jute is produced in handlooms as well as in modern textile mills using state of the art equipment. The fabric is put through the process of *scouring* to remove all traces of natural and added impurities, and is then bleached to remove coloring matter found in the fiber. The bleaching process has to be well regulated as it is lignin which provides color as well as the cementing material. Over-bleaching leads to weakening of the fabric and reduces its value.

## Environmental Concerns

Jute is one of those rare cash crops that are the delight of environmentalists and economists alike. Being a crop grown in mostly developing countries, the methods of farming are still traditional, labor-intensive and old-fashioned, which eliminates high use of chemicals and other pesticides.

In its growing stages, it works as a sponge, absorbing *carbon dioxide* at a greater rate than even trees. Studies show that it absorbs about 15 tons of carbon dioxide and releases 11 tons of *oxygen* in the 100 days of cultivation. Being a rotation crop, after harvesting, it improves the yield of crops planted after it, as large amounts of the leaves and roots are left in the soil leading to natural enrichment. In comparison to trees, which give only about 8 to 10 tons of dry stem per hectare annually, jute gives about 20 to 40 tons.

Jute is a very important geo-textile and is used to make containers that are used in the planting of young trees. Its biodegradability allows for direct planting of the container into the soil and over time the jute degrades naturally. This ensures not only root protection but also reduces labor inputs. In places where soil erosion is a threat, cloth made of jute is draped over the soil preventing erosion while at the same time allowing young plants to breathe and survive. In this application of jute, the ground temperature is also brought down, and the degraded fiber enriches the soil eventually.

## Color/Dyeability

Jute takes on dyes that are compatible with cellulose fiber as it is the cellulosic quality that is the active participant in the dyeing process. Jute is best dyed using reactive dyes that are in consonance with its environmentally friendly qualities. The process is simple and cost-effective while at the same time delivering bright colors with high wash-fastness.

The direct method is cheap and simple, but gives only moderately low wash and moderate to high wash fastness. Sulfur dyeing, although cheap, is a complex process and the shades produced, in spite of their depth, have a dull luster. The vat process is used when the brightness of the fabric is of primary concern. It gives high wash and light fastness, but is expensive and complex. All dyes used in the coloring of jute must show substantivity to the fiber and solubility in water apart from the coloring component.

Soft water is important to the dyeing process because it carries the dye to the surface of the fabric and then through the enlarged pores to its insides. The dyeing process can be done either by exhaustion or padding, with the former being the preferred choice of most manufacturers. The exhaustion method uses a machine called the Jigger, where bundles of fiber are passed back and forth over tubs of dye until the desired color is achieved.

## End Uses

Jute finds myriad uses across all spectrums, from gunny bags used for storing agricultural produce, such as raw cotton, to the finest and most expensive upholstery and draperies. In the carpet making industry, it has been traditionally used as a lining. Jute, being a fancy of designers, also finds a tilt towards exceptional floor coverings in woven, tufted, and piled varieties.

Another great benefit jute offers the environment is through its latest incarnation as a wood fiber, wherein it is used as a non-woven and technical textile. In this form, it is used in the pulp and paper industry, reducing dependence on trees as sources of raw material. This effort directly benefits the environment. In these forms it is also used for underlay, substrate of linoleum, and as fillers in the furniture and bedding industry.

## Jute

Has anti-static qualities
100% biodegradable
Dyes easily
Important geo-textile
Provides good insulation
Intolerant of moisture and humidity
Grows without need for pesticides
Provides natural soil enrichment
Prevents soil erosion
Low thermal conductor

## Characteristics

"I was raised in a family of historic preservationists and conservationists. Additionally, part of formal interior design education is that being a professional designer means being a sustainable designer."

Sarah Barnard, Green Interior Designer
Sarah Barnard Design | sarahbarnarddesign.blogspot.com

# Guide to Green Fabrics™

Eco-friendly textiles for fashion and interior design

guidetogreenfabrics.com

Kenaf

## Overview

Kenaf, which is similar to hemp, is also called Deccan hemp and Java jute, and is extracted specifically from the plant *Hibiscus Cannabinus*, a plant in the Malvaceae family that is related to cotton. It is a member of the hibiscus family, popular among cultivators for endearing and sometimes edible flowers. The fibers obtained from this plant are used mainly in paper products, automobile parts, twine, woven and non-woven fabrics, geo-textiles, and paneling. Like all natural fibers, it is biodegradable and the minimum use of chemicals and other natural resources make it a plant favored for its environmental qualities. The plant's stem produces two types of fibers: bast fibers from the outer layer, and finer fibers from within the core. Kenaf has been used in various applications for over 3 millennia, initially being used to create bags, cordage, and the sails of Egyptian boats.

Also known as a food product, kenaf has been packaged and marketed under the name Gongoora™ in the United States, India, and Korea. It is most commonly consumed by the people of Andhra Pradesh in India where it is a favorite leaf food. In addition, seeds of the plant yield myriad commonly used products. Being a high yielding plant with a low harvesting time makes it ideal for economic and environmental reasons alike. The fact that it sprouts by itself in grasslands and as a weed in wastelands makes it a worthy member of the green fabric contingent.

## Region

Kenaf is native to Africa, but gradually its cultivation has spread to many parts of the globe that have temperate to moist, tropical climates. It is a warm season row crop that grows annually. India is one of the largest producers while other countries where it is cultivated are Bangladesh, Malaysia, South Africa, Mexico, Italy, Spain, the United States, Russia, and the East Asian nations of China, Taiwan, and Indonesia. To a lesser extent, it's grown in southeast Europe where it was introduced in the early 1900's.

## Properties

Kenaf also has characteristics similar to jute. The fibers are pale yellow in color, yet despite this, they are still whiter than the wood pulp used for making paper. It is interesting to note that only about 10% of the fiber is used in the textiles industry. This 10% refers to the thinnest and longest part of the whole fiber, which is then made into yarn used for clothing and home furnishings.

## Production

Kenaf is a bast fiber with the stem of the plant containing the fibers, which are extracted by *decortication* and retting. A fast growing plant of 12 to 14 feet, it takes between 100 and 200 days for the plants to mature. After the plants have been harvested and sorting of the stems done according to thickness, the processing is initiated. Retting is the method of processing kenaf for fiber extraction and can be done either by chemicals or the biological method. To avoid the use of chemicals, kenaf is soaked in running water to loosen the fiber while removing impurities. Ideally, this process is completed in 13 to 15 days from the time the plants are harvested.

Two methods of fiber extraction are followed: single plant extraction and the beat and jerk method. In the single plant extraction method fibers are separated from individual stems generally by hand and kept aside. The fibers obtained in this way are of a very superior quality. In the beat and jerk method about 10 to 12 plants are bundled together and the bottom portion pounded so as to loosen the fibers. The bundle is broken in the center, and with a final jerk, the fiber is removed from the stems. The drawback to this system is that it does not allow for complete extraction of fibers since some fibers remain attached to the stems. The fibers are then laid on bamboo grills to be dried out in the sun for a period of 3 to 4 days, after which they are ready to be sent to factories where they are used for an assortment of purposes. The woody, inner part of the plant inside the stem, the core, is highly valuable as well. Extremely moisture absorbent when used as chips, the core soaks-up four times its weight, unlike traditional wood chips. It is a much more economical option as well.

## Environmental Concerns

One of kenaf's most significant environmental benefits involves its use in the paper industry. Accordingly, in 1960 the United States Department of Agriculture took into account the properties of over 500 plants and found kenaf to be the most promising source for newsprint labeled "tree-free." Traditionally, paper has been made from wood by chopping down trees. Trees are the lungs of the earth and the felling of trees is one of the most damaging factors in *climate change*, second only to the abuse of fossil fuels. By using kenaf for producing paper, trees are spared. This not only positively affects the environment, but also opens newer economic avenues especially in third world countries where it is mostly cultivated. The paper derived from kenaf is also of a much whiter color and this reduces the need to use bleaching agents, leading to fewer adverse impacts on the environment. The energy output in making paper from Kenaf is up to 20% less than what is used with traditional raw materials.

The reasons for kenaf being an environmentally friendly fabric derive not only from its method of cultivation, but more so from the *inherent qualities* of the plant itself. Being akin to a weed, the plant needs minimal care be it in planting, watering, pest management, or harvesting. Due to its hardy nature, it requires a minimum of fertilizers and pesticides. The amount of raw material is relatively higher than what would accrue from a similar acreage of trees, and the cost of production is likewise almost half of what goes into making paper from trees. Kenaf can be called one of the finest and most important members of the green fiber community, and by applying this plant for multifarious functions, humans can greatly reduce negative impact on the ecosystem.

## Color/Dyeability

Kenaf, being a cellulose fiber, can be dyed with vat dyes, naphthol dyes, as well as fiber reactive dyes for smaller scale. Additionally, when kenaf is treated with a commercially available polymer it shows improved dyeability and color fastness properties when dyed with pre-metallised dyes.

## End Uses

Historically, kenaf has been used mainly to produce rope, twine, paper, and coarse cloth, as well as animal bedding and feed. However, in more recent times kenaf fibers have been used in the production of engineered wood, insulation, and clothing-grade cloth. For agricultural purposes, it is used as soil-less potting mix, seeded grass mats for instant lawns, and seeded hydromulch that controls erosion.

kenaf animal bedding

Historically, kenaf has been used mainly to produce rope, twine, paper, and coarse cloth, as well as animal bedding and feed. However, in more recent times kenaf fibers have been used in the production of engineered wood, insulation, and clothing-grade cloth.

Kenaf has been successfully blended with cotton to create a fabric that looks and feels similar to linen, and has the qualities of both linen and cotton. Kenaf is also used as a jute substitute, and when blended with jute, it gives a very strong fabric that is prefect for making bags for transporting and storing grains. In the furnishings industry it is used for making carpet backing. It is extremely handy as packing material, and being a highly absorbent fiber, it is used to soak up liquids and heavy oils. A non-toxic, edible vegetable oil is derived from the seeds of the kenaf plant. High in polyunsaturated fatty acids, kenaf oil helps humans maintain optimum health by reducing heart disease and cholesterol. Multi-purpose in use, this oil also finds its way into cosmetics, and is repurposed as biofuel and industrial lubricants.

## Care

Since most of its clothing related applications involve these fibers being blended with cotton fibers, the fabric will require the same kind of care as cotton fibers, as well as linen. Items may be cleaned in a traditional washing machine or dry-cleaned.

## Kenaf

Extremely absorbent
Biodegradable, returns to the earth in closed-loop fashion
Has characteristics similar to hemp, jute and cotton
Plant produces two types of fibers
Also known as a food product
Sought after as an important geotextile
Requires minimal care to harvest
Leading crop in worldwide paper production
Grows with very little pesticides or fertilizers
Naturally renewable, sprouts independently
Seeds yield myriad, oil-based products
Has pale yellow-colored fibers

## Characteristics

# Designer Spotlight

## Isobel Davies

Eco-fashion pioneer Isobel Davies is the founder and President of Izzy Lane, a cutting edge, unique, ethical luxury brand widely recognized as the leading voice of animal welfare in the fashion industry, as well as for the use of British wool and the British textile industry. Izzy Lane uses wool from its own flock of five hundred rare Wensleydale and Shetland sheep. Her sheep, which have been rescued from slaughter for being – male, missing a pregnancy, being a little lame, being too small, being too old or having imperfections such as a black spot in a white fleece, live out their natural lives in her sheep sanctuary in North Yorkshire. Her collections have shown at London Fashion Week, New York Fashion Week, and in Los Angeles, Berlin, Paris and Milan. Izzy Lane has successful collaborations with Hobbs and Topshop and has shown its collection before the Queen. Its press coverage includes the BBC, ITV, Sky, major print publications, radio, and other national and international press. Izzy Lane's commitment to the animals, as well as the fibers they produce, is what sets it apart. "Until I started Izzy Lane, I found no evidence that there was any traceability of animal fibers in the fashion industry. It was the beginnings of the ethical fashion movement, but animals were not considered part of the equation. Questions were being asked of where our food was coming from and in terms of meat, whether the animal had had a good life, but the same could not be said of the animal which produced the fiber for our jumper," says Isobel. She further states, "All of our production is within a 150 km radius. From where we nurture the sheep, to the scourer, the dyer, the spinner, and the weaver, the miles are kept to an absolute minimum. Izzy Lane is fairly unique in the ethical fashion space, however, our main raison d'etre is to promote animal welfare through a luxury clothing line. It is at the core of everything we do." Wool is Isobel's favorite fiber. She explains, "Shetland sheep were brought to the UK in the 11th century by the Vikings. They are a remarkable, small, primitive breed with fine, soft wool similar to cashmere. There are 13 distinct colors such as rust colored moorit and grey katmoget. A lot of our wool is used, woven into cloth in their natural colors in the traditional Victorian mills - herringbones, hopsacks, houndtooths. Wensleydales have a long, curly lustrous fleece which is like silk." In Isobel's words, fashion dictates fashion, it is high-profile and speaks to the next generation - our future. "We cannot continue to pollute the earth, our seas, destroy wildlife habitats, use up our finite natural resources, and imagine there will be no consequences. The fashion industry needs an internal revolution to adopt a philosophy of respect and sustainability," she says. Isobel says she has faith in next generation, "They are the building blocks of our future and they are more aware, less self-orientated, and more proactive than mine. As they take their places in industry, then I believe it will change."

Izzy Lane Ltd | izzylane.com

soybeans and soy milk

Milk fiber has humectant properties that make the skin smooth and delicate, and the amino acids present make it anti-fungal and anti-bacterial. The fiber has a wonderful suppleness about it enhanced by a gloss giving it a superbly luxurious feel similar to silk. It also offers superior strength.

"Fashion dictates fashion, it is high-profile and it talks to the next generation
- our future. We cannot continue to pollute the earth, our seas, destroy wildlife
habitats, use up our finite natural resources, and imagine there will be no
consequences. The fashion industry needs an internal revolution to adopt a
philosophy of respect and sustainability."

Isobel Davies, Green Fashion Designer
Izzy Lane Ltd | izzylane.com

# Guide to
## Green Fabrics™
### Eco-friendly textiles for fashion and interior design

guidetogreenfabrics.com

# Milk Protein

## Overview

The world in which we live is so technologically advanced that nothing seems an impossibility to us. We would not disbelieve the achievement of actual fabric production from milk, which is happening all around us this very moment. Fabric made from milk protein is not only a reality, but is well on its way to being an answer to many of the skin problems that plague millions of people in a world that is slowly losing its protective *ozone layer*.

Milk protein, as it is known, gives the wearer almost the same benefits that come from ingesting the liquid. These positive benefits are the result of the 18 amino acids contained in milk in its liquid form also being found in the fabric. The amino acids nourish the skin, protecting it from allergens, and reportedly go a long way in postponing the onset of wrinkles.

The skin improving qualities of milk have been known to man from ancient times and the beauty of Cleopatra was credited to the milk bath, one of her favorite indulgences. This may have been the secret behind her flawless complexion. In modern times, we may not be able to soak in a tub full of milk, but nothing can prevent us from wearing it and getting the same benefits as the Egyptian queen. China is the leading producer of milk protein fiber. It is a very refreshing fabric to wear due to its high breathability and extreme absorption properties. Milk fiber was invented in the 1930's in America and Italy, and was known as ARALAC™, Lanatil™, and Merinova™. It received a stamp of approval in April 2004 when it was awarded the International Ecological Textile Oeko-Tex Standard 100 Authentication.

## Properties

Milk fiber has humectant properties that make the skin smooth and delicate, and the amino acids present make it anti-fungal and anti-bacterial. The fiber has a wonderful suppleness about it enhanced by a gloss giving it a superbly luxurious feel similar to silk. It also offers superior strength.

Milk fiber assimilates well with wool and cashmere on account of its three-dimensional and multi-gap structure, making the blended fabric extremely lightweight and heat retentive. It is ideal wear for the cold season. When blended with cotton and cashmere and used for making high-quality undergarments, its amino acids and natural wet protecting genes keep the wearer free from fungal infections and other such conditions.

## Production

The process of turning liquid milk into fabric involves *dewatering* it, wherein the water content of the milk is removed to get it ready for *skimming*. The skimmed milk is then turned into a protein spinning fluid that makes it suitable for the wet spinning process by application of advanced engineering techniques. During the spinning process micro zinc ions are embedded in the fiber, which imparts to it the quality of being *bacteriostatic* as well as increasing its durability. Formaldehyde is not used in the production process, therefore contributing to its green standing.

## Environmental Concerns

By itself or used in blends, milk protein fiber may be the answer to some of our skin related problems. Apart from the processing of the fiber, which necessitates energy consumption, and perhaps transportation, there are no other negative environmental impacts. Due to these factors it is indeed one of the finest examples of a green fabric.

## Color/Dyeability

Milk fibers tend to be colorfast and absorb dyes very easily creating a huge palette of shades from the brightest to the lightest. It can be dyed using reactive, cationic, and acidic dyes.

## End Uses

Milk fibers are best used when blended with natural fibers such as cashmere, cotton, silk, wool, or ramie. It is used most often to make undergarments for the young and old, as well as to make clothes for newborns and children as it nourishes the skin and prevents allergies and rashes. It combines with different fibers in different ways to create extraordinarily beautiful new fabrics. When used in conjunction with bamboo rayon, milk fiber offers better moisture retention qualities as well as better wicking properties. This keeps the wearer cool and elegant even in the most humid of conditions.

## Care

Considered an easy care fabric, milk protein is easily washable in a washing machine on normal settings. Care instructions should be followed, and fabric blends taken into account to preserve the fabric. Dry on normal settings or dry clean.

## Milk Protein

Extremely absorbent
Has 18 amino acids that nourish skin
Anti-bacterial
Anti-fungal
Has high breathability qualities
Colorfast, offering lovely, bright colors
Very durable and strong
Lightweight yet heat retentive
Has good moisture retention and wicking qualities
Offers superior strength
Very supple and soft, akin to silk
Has natural, wet protecting genes

## Characteristics

# Guide to Green Fabrics™

Eco-friendly textiles for fashion and interior design

guidetogreenfabrics.com

Modal

## Overview

A fabric similar to rayon, Modal is one of the newest fabrics to make a striking impact on the fashion and home décor industries. However, it differs from rayon in that rayon is produced from the chips of any tree, while Modal uses only Beech wood chips. It is a 100% cellulosic bio-fiber made completely by human ingenuity propelled by the desire to make maximum use of available resources found all around us. Modal is the industry name for *modacrylic fiber*. Its formal name is Lenzing Modal®, a registered trademark of Lenzing AG™, an Austrian company specializing in textiles and fibers, particularly natural fibers made from cellulose.

Using chips of the Beech wood tree exclusively, the fiber is an amalgamation of the benefits found in natural fibers and enhanced by the extremely soft feel of synthetic fibers. Like natural fibers, it has the capacity for extreme water absorption and breathability. With this, it combines elegant drape, softness of touch, and high levels of comfort and wearability, which are the hallmarks of man-made fibers.

## Properties

Modal glides like real silk over skin surfaces glowing with a bright luster, which is retained even after continuous washing. Unlike natural garments, it tends to be resistant to creasing leading to a relatively lesser amount of care needed to maintain the fabric. Modal is abrasion free and does not *pill*. The smooth texture of the fabric prevents the deposition of lime on the surface even when washed with hard water, and thus keeps the fabric as soft as it was when first used. It does not lose its shape even upon becoming wet and will not shrink. It is highly *hygroscopic* (water absorbent), extremely supple, and will not fade. The fabric is known for its durability and long-lasting qualities.

## Production

Modal is made from reconstituted cellulose and the production involves pulping the wood, involving it in a chemical process using soda solution, spinning it into yarn, and finally processing it into high-quality cellulose fabric. The fiber is used most often as a blend, usually with cotton, since the two have similar qualities.

## Environmental Concerns

From the point of energy consumption, the production process necessitates considerable energy inputs in comparison to those needed for producing natural fibers. What works in its favor, however, is the fact that it is made from wooden chips taken from trees that have a long life and are also used in a manner that is consistent with sustainable agricultural practices. Because it is a fiber whose raw material is sourced from Beech wood trees, the amount of fertilizers, pesticides, and water requirement is minimal in keeping with the tenets of environmentally friendly practices. The timber used in production is generally that which has been rejected for use in making furniture, flooring, and other construction items. It is a 100% biodegradable fabric despite the fact that it is man-made.

## Color/Dyeability

During the dyeing process, Modal behaves almost the same as cotton. When using reactive dyes and processing 100% cotton yarns plus Modal in a single fabric, this leads to a unique two-color effect. This allows for greater design independence, especially in terry fabrics where Modal is often used as a blend. Modal fabrics are often dyed using either the piece dyeing or yarn dyeing method and has the ability to showcase a wide range of colors.

## End Uses

The modern fashion industry finds modal fabric extremely pliable and well suited for creating garments that need to be light, elegant, and rich in hand. Luxurious bed sheets, towels, and bathrobes are created from this fiber. Even after repeated usage the fabric wrinkles only slightly calling for very low maintenance.

Its use in creating beautiful lingerie is unrivaled not only because of its lightness and color, but also because of its inherent elasticity and high absorption. Micromodal, a micro variant, is the finest cellulose fiber, and is so light that ten thousand meters of the fiber weigh just one gram. This fabric is used to create high-end luxury clothing for consumers worldwide.

## Care

Fabrics that are made of 100% modal need to be lightly ironed after washing, but apart from this there are no other major care concerns. Even when washed in warm water it retains its vibrant color, but low temperature washing is recommended. It has sensitivity to chlorine bleach, which should be used in minimal amounts. The fabric should be dried according to directions, which likely will be similar to those for drying cotton.

## Modal

Abrasion-free, does not pill
Extremely absorbent, up to 50% more than cotton
100% biodegradable
Has excellent breathability characteristics
100% cellulosic bio fiber
Has high levels of comfort
Offers elegant drape and softness like silk
Durable and long lasting
High elasticity
Not susceptible to fading, extremely colorfast
Highly hygroscopic
Has bright luster
Has sensitivity to chlorine bleach
Resistant to creasing, does not easily wrinkle

## Characteristics

"I felt the (fashion) industry on the whole does more harm than good in its production methods, and that the earth was suffering and needed help. So I wanted to do my part. I have been using recycled materials for almost 30 years, way before it was cool or there was an "eco conscious" name for it. It's a lifestyle choice for me."

Deborah Lindquist, Green Fashion Designer
Deborah Lindquist Eco Fashion Brand | deborahlindquist.com

# Guide to Green Fabrics™

## Eco-friendly textiles for fashion and interior design

guidetogreenfabrics.com

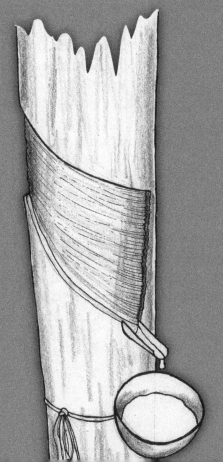

## Natural Latex

## Overview

Latex is a generic term coined by Charles Marie de la Condamine from the Latin word "latex," meaning fluid. It refers to the milky, sap-like fluid found in many plants that is a combination of alkaloids, proteins, sugars, starch, resins, tannins, and gum. A sticky mixture indeed, latex is organically designed to ward off natural predators, but has also found its way into the consumer spotlight.

Natural latex harvesting and production mainly takes place in Thailand, Indonesia, Malaysia, and Sri Lanka, all located in Southeast Asia. Historically, Brazil was a major producer and the originator of the rubber tree. In 1876, a local planter, Henry Wickham, exported seeds from Brazil to the United Kingdom on behalf of the British government. The seeds were germinated in London shortly thereafter. Eventually, seeds were exported to Sri Lanka, and in 1877, twenty-two seedlings made their way to Singapore, took root, and the tapping technique for latex extraction became standard. Prior to tapping, rubber trees (*hevea brasiliensis*) were routinely felled to extract natural latex, which is made from the liquid that oozes from it when the bark of the plant is slashed, or *tapped*, about every 2 days. However, the liquid is not sap, which is located deeper within the tree, but derives from latex ducts, which are in a layer immediately outside the *cambium*.

In order for the tree to continue to grow in a healthy manner, the tree's cambium must remain intact. If it becomes cut, the tree is considered damaged and will not grow nor produce latex since the cambium is where tree growth takes place. Slashes are made on the tree's trunk by skillful workers called tappers, and a cup suspended at the bottom catches the dripping, milky substance. As evidenced, the liquid has a tendency to coagulate when exposed to air unless treated with a stabilizing agent such as ammonia. Regarding controlled growth, rubber tree plantations are common in the aforementioned countries, as are smaller groves termed *smallholdings*. Science is involved toward ensuring genetically identical trees in order to produce a pure product each and every time. This is done through a process called *bud grafting*.

## Properties

Natural latex is hypo-allergenic with anti-microbial properties as well as being mite resistant. It also has excellent breathable qualities and tends to be cool in summer and warm in winter. It's this property of natural latex that makes it a preferred choice for mattresses along with its natural cushioning properties. Natural latex is non-toxic as well as biodegradable. It is used to make certain garments, which need to fit the body like a second skin. Latex is produced by more than 20,000 species of plants, but the rubber made from most is unsuitable for commercial uses.

## Production

Extreme care must be taken to extract natural latex from the rubber tree, and only skilled tappers can handle this task. Beginning around dawn, tappers use sharp knives to shave off sections of bark. Needing to be micro-thin, the shavings and cuts must be near the surface of the tree, and not too thick. The tree's ability to live depends on this level of accuracy. Once cut, the latex flows, finding its way into a small cup placed underneath the cut by the tapper. After a few hours, the tapper returns to collect the latex, either treated or untreated, and prepares it for processing. *Rubber* is the product that results in latex not being treated with ammonia. It is used for a wide variety of purposes in its own right.

Natural latex is further processed by straining and then it is concentrated. As a benefit, proteins remain in natural latex because heat is not used for its production. Next, another dose of stabilizer is added and some of the water is removed by a process called *centrifuging*. The result is natural latex concentrate and contains approximately 40% water and proteins, and 60% rubber. The collected resin is later whipped and baked in order to make it ready for consumer use. A familiar product, latex gloves, are made from natural latex concentrate.

## Environmental Concerns

As a plus to sustainability, natural latex is collected without damaging the environment since there is no felling of trees or harvesting of leaves or fruits. The tree is used years on end for its natural offerings and is thus a long-term asset to the environment. Generally, latex is white in color, but some plants give out a yellow, orange, or even scarlet colored liquid. It has extremely low dye acceptance and often is used in its naturally colored state.

## End Uses

Natural latex is often used in conjunction with other fibers to create novel materials with specialized uses. Due to its highly waterproof nature, it is frequently used for occupations where working in close proximity to water is unavoidable. By wearing gloves made of latex, the skin is protected from excessive and unnecessary exposure to water. Hygiene products, especially for use in hospitals, are made from natural latex and these include catheters and gloves. Its other applications include use in foundation garments, socks, armor, and soles.

## Care

Caring for latex products is not time consuming, but certain precautions and procedures need to be followed. Garments made from latex should be rinsed clean in warm water and then hung upside down to be dried. Use of solvents is not advised as the chemicals contained in them may lead to breakdown of the chemical composition of natural latex and render the garment useless. The fiber also lacks resistance to oxidizing agents and can be damaged by oil, sunlight, perspiration, and aging. Therefore, natural latex garments should be stored in a cool, dry place away from sunlight.

## Natural Latex

Has anti-microbial properties
100% biodegradable
Excellent breathability qualities, cool in summer
Coagulates when exposed to air unless treated
White, yellow, orange or scarlet colored
Damaged by oil, sunlight, perspiration and aging
Has extremely low dye acceptance
Naturally hypo-allergenic and non-toxic
Inherently mite resistant
Warm in winter
High waterproof nature

## Characteristics

"People will have to continually recommit to a sustainable lifestyle because it is easy to make those choices that are not green."

Sarah Barnard, Green Interior Designer
Sarah Barnard Design | sarahbarnarddesign.blogspot.com

# Guide to Green Fabrics™

Eco-friendly textiles for fashion and interior design

guidetogreenfabrics.com

# Organic Cashmere

## Overview

The mere mention of the word "cashmere" and the mind conjures up images of cold, chilly weather, and being wrapped up in the warm, buttery folds of one of the world's most luxurious fabrics. The deep warmth of this fiber belies its softness and lightness, which keeps the wearer warm without bulkiness like other woolens. The word is an Anglicization of the word *Kashmir*, an Indian state, which is an important source of the wool. Shawls made of cashmere have been used by people for more than two millennia and written records from the 3rd B.C. document its use.

Systematic production of the fabric is credited to Zyn-ul-Abidin, a 15th century Kashmir royal, who brought in weavers from Turkistan to create exotic designs. Europeans were treated to the beauty and softness of this warm fabric when a French General, fighting in the French campaigns in Egypt during the wars between 1799 and 1812, sent home a shawl made of cashmere. From then on, the clamor for cashmere began, which continues unabated till date.

Cashmere fibers are taken from the undercoat of the cashmere goat, scientifically known as *Capra hircus langier*. The goat has a double fleece, with the outer layer of coarse hair hiding the valuable soft undercoat. When the goat moults during spring, which coincides in the Northern Hemisphere between the months of March to May, shepherds get down to the arduous task of collecting the fiber and separating it from the coarse upper hair in a process called *dehairing*. It is important to note how cashmere goats are raised, paying particular attention to their feeding and grazing methods, to determine if in fact one is purchasing organic cashmere as opposed to traditional cashmere. For reasons of environmental concern, holistic fiber production methods will also need to apply.

## Region

Cashmere goats are reared as livestock by the people of Central Asia, India, China, Scotland, Afghanistan, Turkey, Ladakh, Iran, Kazakhstan, Kyrgyzstan, Inner Mongolia, Tajikistan, Uzbekistan, and Turkmenistan. China ranks first in the production of cashmere followed by Mongolia, Afghanistan, and Iran, and China indeed produces the finest and most expensive cashmere in the world. It is also produced in the United States in limited quantities. Scotland boasts incredibly soft and luxurious spun yarns that are used for sweaters and shawls, in particular, paisley shawls. Cashmere is a scarce commodity and only about 15,000 tons are produced annually. The Cashmere and Camel Hair Manufacturers Institute sets definitions and standards for this fiber internationally, and the Wool Products Labeling Act of 1939 sets labeling standards in the United States. The quality of cashmere depends upon its diameter and the international accepted standard is anything below 19 microns in weight and a minimum length of 1.25 inches. Fibers weighing 16 microns or less constitute the premium quality and are a designer's delight.

## Properties

There is much difficulty in conceiving a perfect fiber that offers myriad qualities that would rank it extremely high on the fashion radar. It would need to possess numerous, outstanding characteristics for wide appeal, thus commanding a higher than normal market revenue share as an added benefit. Such as a genie offering only one wish, organic cashmere appears to have magically fulfilled such requirements, and on a global scale.

This naturally *crimpy*, durable fiber transforms itself constantly to surface as solid wardrobe investments the world over. Easily, cashmere garments and accessories can literally last a lifetime and are seen as rare gems. Due to its inherent qualities and natural production and processing methods, the fiber is lustrous, smooth, and pill-free. Organic cashmere fabric is warm and comforting and has tiny, insulating air-spaces found between the fibers. A wrinkle-free fabric, cashmere also keeps the body cool. Described as the most luxurious fiber ever, many fashionable items are made from organic cashmere and are finding ways into luxury retail establishments on every continent.

## Production

The removal of the *down* is sometimes done by running a coarse comb over the fleece of the goat, which results in greater amounts of pure cashmere being retrieved. The coarse hair obtained is used for other applications, generally in brushes, upholstery, floor coverings, and inter-linings, while soft fibers are used for fine garments. The first step in the preparation of the fiber is called *sorting* whereby fibers are sorted by grade and color. Next, fibers are *scoured* to remove dirt, animal grease, sand, vegetable matter and various impurities. The fibers are then prepared for dehairing and will be machine processed to further sort the fibers by class: fine, soft underdown, and coarse guard hair. Various dehairing heads on the machine sort the mass of fiber into the correct categories for processing. Economically speaking, the goal of dehairing is to maintain the integrity and length of the underdown while removing most of the coarse hair and impurities.

In its uncolored state the fiber is found in shades of brown, gray, and white and these are then dyed mostly by hand using metal-free and azo-free dyes. The wool absorbs color quickly and these colors give a rich look to the fabric. The fibers are soaked in vats of color for a fixed amount of time after which they are dried to prepare for spinning. Excess moisture can weaken the strength of the fiber and so a *hydro-extractor* is often used to remove excess moisture. After dehairing and dyeing, the fiber is considered processed and is ready to be sent to spinners, knitters and weavers worldwide. The *spinning* process uses an oil application to allow for fibers to stick to each other, which after spinning is washed off with water. The fiber is generally spun by hand.

Woolen yarn will be made from the processed fiber using the *woolen yarn system*. However, worsted yarn, being the top commodity it is, will see its fibers pass through one final step: *combing*. This integrates it into the *worsted yarn system*. With a goal of arranging the fibers into parallel form, the cashmere fibers are combed to retain the longest fibers while short fibers are removed. Known as *top*, the longer, parallel fibers can then be spun into worsted yarns. The remaining short fiber is called *noil*. From there, the yarns are either knitted into garments or woven into cloth. The weaving process is almost always done by hand. The extremely delicate nature of the fiber cannot withstand the vibrations caused by power looms. By either method, the resultant fabric is always quite luxurious.

## Environmental Concerns

There are a number of important and environmentally friendly practices observed in the production of organic cashmere. From what cashmere goats eat to how they eat it and how their hair is manufactured, natural processes must be adhered-to in order for a green label to apply.

Low maintenance in nature, the goats are allowed to range and graze freely on chemical-free pasture that does not contain hormones or toxins. During manufacturing, dirt and grease found in the hair is largely removed with water. Toxic chemicals are not necessary to these production methods. In addition, producers who observe more holistic methods of doing business understand environmental impact and therefore develop methods to advance their organic standing. Part of this observation results in laborious practices, which further result in premium costs for this particular fiber, which tends to be quite pure. However, producers may also integrate controls on storage, transportation, energy use, and water systems while employing fair working conditions for employees, thus rounding out the overall eco-production cycle.

## End Uses

Cashmere is used for making a variety of products, mostly for use in the apparel and furnishings industries. The softest form of cashmere is called *pashmina* and derives from the Persian word for wool, called *pashm*. While other cashmeres and cashmere blends may pass as pashmina, true pashmina cashmere comes from the fleece of several specific mountain goat breeds, including Changthangi (from Kashmir, India), Chyangra (from Nepal), and Kaghani (from Pakistan). Cashmere is a high-end luxury product and it is used to make sweaters, shawls, scarves, jackets, hats, coats, suits, socks, and gloves of the softest quality, yet it stays extremely warm and comforting. It is also used to make lightweight blankets, quilts, and throws, among other luxury products.

## Care

Cashmere apparel boasts exotic beauty and extreme versatility of use. Garments are akin to heirlooms and expensive cashmere is handed down from generation to generation. It is a legacy that has to be well cared for and looked after. It is best to keep cashmere away from any obvious conditions that could soil it. In case it gets dirty, washing the soiled area in cold water by hand using a fine, washable soap is best followed by dry cleaning, the preferred cleaning method for cashmere. However, if washing by machine, be sure the machine does not have an agitator during the hand wash or wool cycles. Cashmere should not be wrung-out to get rid of excess water as this may distort the shape of the garment. Instead, it may be rolled in a towel and pressed for excess water, then laid flat to dry, away from heat or direct sunlight. When dry, it should be brushed with the nap. Cashmere can be ironed when it is slightly damp on a cool setting by using a *press cloth*, which will preserve the fabric's qualities. Ironing should be done on the wrong side, or back side, of the garment. Unfortunately, a hot iron can scorch the fibers permanently.

Because cashmere is a protein fiber it should not be washed using any kind of chlorine bleach as this leads to loss of color, permanent yellowing, and weakening of the fiber. In fact, it will dissolve in bleach so it's best to avoid it entirely. The fabric must also be protected against friction if at all possible. For example, it should not be sandwiched between the wearer and any surface, such as an armrest or piece of furniture. To store cashmere garments, use tissue paper for knitwear laying flat in a drawer to avoid hanging. Woven garments may be hung on padded hangers, and to preserve the shape, buttons and zippers should be fastened. Wrinkles will generally disappear when garments are given a rest. If garments are to be stored for a season, they should be grouped in a loose garment bag and stored in a cool, dry place. Knits may be stored in a drawer and moth crystals or spray will help control moths. As evidenced, extreme care is urged for the preservation of one of the most luscious fibers available to the marketplace today.

## Organic Cashmere

Has natural crimp
Super durable and sturdy
Very insulating and warm
Long-lasting
Has high luster
Highly luxurious fiber
Does not pill
Rare, therefore expensive
Smooth hand
Softens with age, builds character
Does not wrinkle

## Characteristics

Hand painted details on bamboo rayon pillows by Kristene Smith

organic cotton shopping bag

Large companies like Nike™ are blending organic cotton with other fibers to slowly attune customers to the superiority of the fibers, leading to greater demands that will slowly propel all cotton farming towards organic methods of cultivation.

"Conventional cotton uses more than 25% of the world's chemical pesticides and fertilizers, making it the number one most pesticide laden crop in the USA. These pesticides are extremely toxic and pollute groundwater while endangering wildlife and plant species."

Beth Doane, Green Fashion Designer
RainTees | raintees.com

# Guide to Green Fabrics™

Eco-friendly textiles for fashion and interior design

guidetogreenfabrics.com

## Organic Cotton

## Overview

Annual production of traditional cotton stands at around 10 million metric tons, and so the amount of harmful pesticides and fertilizers used in its cultivation number staggering amounts. Unfortunately, by reducing even a small percentage of these harmful chemicals, the impact on the environment is still plentiful. With traditional cotton production, there are issues of soil toxicity and run-off of harmful chemicals into waterways, among other environmental concerns. Fortunately, the contagious zeal of environmentalists, sustainable farmers, and conscientious consumers paved the way for finding newer methods of growing cotton without the use of harmful pesticides and fertilizers. In fact, organic cotton production began as a result of these concerted efforts. The harvesting and production of organic cotton is an extremely ethical enterprise, and the regulations that govern certification of cotton as organic are so stringent that total environmental benefits can be visibly maintained. These innovative production methods ensure not only elimination of hazardous chemical substances, but at the same time replenish the soil making it more fertile and productive.

## Region

Organic cotton is cultivated in the United States, Turkey, India, China, Africa, Peru, Uganda, Tanzania, Egypt, Senegal, and Israel, and many other countries. Farmers realizing its benign impact on the environment exhibit an obvious, global shift toward growing cotton organically.

## Properties

Because of the lack of chemical processing involved, organic cotton has wonderful drape, hand, and textural qualities that enhance the look and feel of garments. These untreated fabrics have a matte luster with enhanced smoothness. The fabric retains its natural wax resulting in its smooth hand, which in traditional cotton fabrics is stripped away during processing. This untreated fabric has more weight leading to elegant drape and excellent fall. Further, by eliminating the dyeing process and using naturally colored organic cotton, the cost is also considerably less, while it is a boon for people who suffer from allergies caused by dyes.

## Production/ Environmental Concerns

There are numerous, important steps on the path to achieving the highest standards in organic cotton production. Needing to be followed closely to ensure a proper product, farmers across the globe are working in concert for the benefit of consumers seeking a greener horizon, indeed the hallmark of a clean legacy for generations to come. To begin, changes to farming conditions must be evidenced to receive an organic stamp of approval. For three years, organic fields must be cleansed and free of any prohibited substances prior to planting. Physical barriers and buzzers also need to be installed for the protection of organic crops, which must be maintained separately from chemically intensive crops and surface run-off. Soil fertility must also be promoted by farmers, and the biological, chemical, and physical condition of the soil should minimize erosion. In the USA, the United States Department of Agriculture's National Organic Program (NOP) sets these stringent standards. Through a very involved process, organic cotton production continues with seed preparation. This is an important early-stage step. Dismissing the use of toxic fungicides and insecticides common in conventional cotton processing, organic cotton seeds are natural and pesticide free. Genetically Modified Organisms (GMO's) are never used.

Many moons ago, farmers instinctively used crop rotation as a means of soil enrichment, fertility, retention, and pest control. In essence, pests, weeds, and disease could no longer anticipate the same plantings over and over, therefore, the soil became used to the receipt of organic matter and fresh crops that enriched it, freeing the soil from mundane and routine usage that drained nutrients.

As society advanced and economics became more of a factor in business and everyday life, farmers moved to a mono-crop culture meaning they planted single crops on vast amounts of land to yield more revenue. With this, products to control weeds, disease, and pests were desperately needed because crop rotation had ceased. Although the introduction of synthetic pesticides brought relief, also present were toxic chemicals that remained in the crops, spilled into waterways, and damaged the soil leaving it extremely nutrient deficient. Organic cotton farming uses the crop-rotation method only, and takes us back to the beginning where *biodiversity* and holistic methods of crop enhancement were employed for local benefit. With weed control being a major consideration, organic cotton production involves hand removal of weeds instead of toxic herbicides used with conventional cotton. With hand removal, chemicals are not present and therefore never airborne. Hoeing by hand is another method used to keep weeds under control. With these methods, a fair amount of human capital is necessary to grow and manage organic cotton, thus resulting in higher prices.

With pests continuously lurking, innovation to employ new pest management techniques is high on the list. Through healthy soil maintenance and deliberate integration of beneficial insects, such as ladybugs, farmers give themselves a good running start. Biological practices, cultural tactics, and a little trickery also assist. As an example, a pest's second favorite crop may be planted slightly away from the organic cotton to lure it in the opposite direction, sparing it sure damage. This presents a natural balance in pest control and sends a nod to creative thinking in modern farming. With traditional cotton production using almost 25% of worldwide insecticide consumption, new methods of control were desperately needed. Not to mention the high toxicity associated with aerial spraying that harms workers, communities, animals, and other farms.

For *defoliation*, or the removal of leaves from the cotton plant, to occur naturally, organic cotton farmers use seasonal tactics like freezing temperatures for control. Water management is another method that helps with leaf removal so that toxic chemicals do not have to be introduced into the scenario. However, toxic chemicals continue to be used in traditional cotton cultivation for defoliation. Finally, rich, healthy soil contributes to water retention, and organic cotton absorbs plenty of water so there is no shortage there. What's unique about watering organic cotton is its lower amount of run-off due to retention, and lack of harmful chemicals in the water that does run off.

## Color/Dyeability

Dyes that color traditional cotton impact the environs negatively by using excessive water, chemicals, electricity output, and other mechanical add-ons for energy purposes. There are many alternatives such as natural dyes, which produce striking colors on organic cotton. For example, vegetables dyes offer an abundance of hues using everyday products found at home or in local markets. Simple dyeing methods include boiling dyestuffs and straining them, adding a fixative such as salt or vinegar (if desired), and soaking the fabric to desired result.

In addition, with great scientific research and application of newer ways of cultivation, naturally colored organic cotton has emerged and is grown on the stem, eliminating the need for the dyeing process completely. However, the range of colors at present is restricted to brown, reddish-brown, green, and yellow. Unlike dyed cotton, which fades with washing, naturally colored organically grown cotton exhibits a propensity towards deepening of color during its first three washes.

## End Uses

Due to its higher cost, organic cotton is generally used to make high-end garments and accessories for discerning customers. Home furnishings designers show increased propensity toward incorporating organic cotton as it is hypo-allergenic and highly suitable for bed sheets, bedcovers, duvets, and towels. It is also used to make baby clothes, diapers, and baby blankets.

Large companies like Nike™ are blending organic cotton with other fibers to slowly attune customers to the superiority of the fibers, leading to greater demands that will slowly propel all cotton farming towards organic methods of cultivation. It is only market demand that will create greater exposure of organic cotton products, which will help ensure that our planet remains clean and green.

## Care

Organic cotton gets its green stamp of approval primarily due to elimination of dangerous chemical applications during cultivation and processing. Therefore, with cultivating organic cotton human input is increased, which leads to limited production and higher costs. This is why organic cotton is a niche product, and so taking care of these expensive items is also integral to the choice process. Better care in the initial stages can extend the life of an organic cotton garment. During the first wash the addition of ¼ cup of vinegar to the water in the final rinse ensures that these items retain their color and will not bleed. It is a good practice to wash these garments inside out using mild detergent without bleach. Organic cotton clothes are best dried away from direct sunlight since it may cause shrinkage, a problem inherent in all natural fibers.

## Organic Cotton

100% biodegradable
Employs the crop rotation method only
Becomes slightly darker with subsequent washings
Offers wonderful drape
Takes well to natural dyes (including vegetable)
Genetically Modified Organisms (GMO's)
are never used
Has superior hand and textural qualities
Has matte luster with enhanced smoothness
Retains its natural wax
Naturally colored varieties also available
Dismisses the use of harmful pesticides and fertilizers
Naturally replenishes soil, prevents erosion
Weightier, has elegant drape and excellent fall

## Characteristics

# Designer Spotlight

## Deborah Lindquist

As one of Los Angeles' most sought after environmentally conscious designers, Deborah Lindquist creates exquisite apparel, accessories, and home-décor pieces out of a mix of recycled and new sustainable and organic fabrics. Originally trained at Parsons School of Design in New York City, she eventually moved her business to Los Angeles and began successfully catering to hip, young urbanites and boutiques throughout the US, Canada, Europe, and Asia. Today, Deborah's eco-conscious clothing line combines environmental responsibility with a cutting-edge aesthetic. As noted in fashion magazines and blogs around the world, she works her fashion magic with a mixture of eco-conscious fabrications (from vintage cashmere and hemp blends to organic linen) and the resulting designs are as striking as they are ecologically sensitive. She has dressed such mega-stars as Sharon Stone, Pink, Jessica Alba, Christina Aguilera, Rihanna and many other celebrities. Her work has been featured in the Huffington Post, LA Times, Elle, Lucky, In Style, WWD, LA Brides, Ecouterre, Good Morning America, and many other shows and publications. Deborah describes her eco-consciousness, "I felt the (fashion) industry as a whole does more harm than good in its production methods, and that the earth was suffering and needed help so I wanted to do my part. I've been using recycled materials for almost 30 years, way before it was cool or there was an "eco conscious" name for it. It's a lifestyle choice for me including my food and product choices." She uses a blend of recycled, organic, and sustainable fabrics: organic linen, organic cotton, hemp, modal-silk blends; and recycled materials such as cashmere, kimono, sari, leather, lace and wool. Hemp is her favorite fabric. All of her products are locally made, which contributes to her ideals of hiring and producing locally. Deborah acknowledges the limits green fabric manufacturing has, especially in the U.S., but believes that long-term, grass roots methods can occur within the textiles industry. She also understands the need for more farmers who are willing to grow organic and sustainable crops. "Creating awareness has to be somewhat entertaining to capture anyone's attention and it has to make sense in people's lives. Since you're talking about the fashion industry and not just the fabrics, that has to be included too," she states. Deborah's top five suggestions for creating awareness of the importance of green fabrics: creating a story about green fabrics and their origins, developing stronger and more durable eco-fabrics for quality control, better promotion of the benefits of going green, creating awareness about local artisans and green designers, and developing fashionable garments for the public.

Photographer: Chika Okazumi
Model: Amy Rose, MUA Eugene Conde

Photographer: Autumn Stankay
Model: Alexandra Naples

Photographer: Glenn Campbell
Model: Maria Berlinder, MUA Mitzi Gip

organic linen fabric

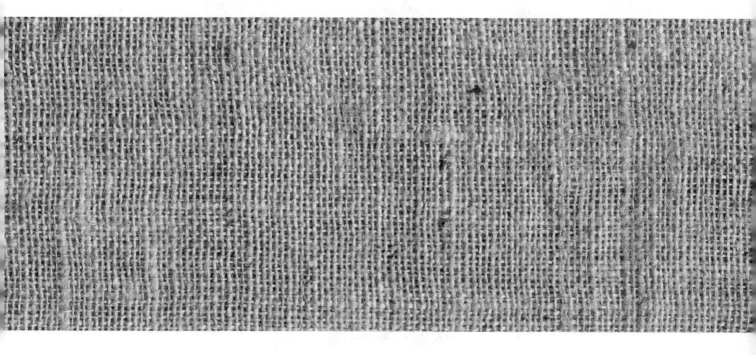

Linen has a wide range of characteristics which makes it preferred
wear especially during summertime. It has a natural lightness
along with an inherent stiffness, which keeps the fabric from
clinging to the skin.

"I use a blend of recycled, organic, and sustainable fabrics including organic linen and organic cotton - both are beneficial since no pesticide or herbicide is used to pollute the environment."

Deborah Lindquist, Green Fashion Designer
Deborah Lindquist Eco Fashion Brand | deborahlindquist.com

# Guide to Green Fabrics ™

**Eco-friendly textiles for fashion and interior design**

guidetogreenfabrics.com

# Organic Linen

## Overview

When the tombs of Egypt's Pharaohs were opened and the mummies discovered, archaeologists found that the mummies had been wrapped in swathes of linen, and both the bodies and the fabric were found to be well preserved. This reveals that linen had been around for more than 6 millennia, and that it was a fiber being widely used by humans throughout the ages. Linen is indeed the oldest fiber known to man and the first used in the production of clothing. The flax plant is the actual plant from which linen fibers come, therefore linen is often referred to as *flax*. The fabric was introduced to European nations through the Phoenicians who carried on a thriving trade in the fiber. The cool, fresh, and light touch of linen on the skin makes it the preferred choice in warm climates, while its beautiful texture and subtle sheen endear it to almost all people. When organic methods of cultivation apply, it is referred to as organic linen.

## Region

Centuries ago, flax was grown mainly in the Nile delta, but now the largest producers of this plant are the European nations of France, Belgium, and the Netherlands. These are the largest linen fabric producers as well. The other significant producers of this crop are China and Russia. Italy and Ireland also grow flax and produce some of the best quality linen fabric for use in high-quality products.

## Properties

Linen has a wide range of characteristics which makes it preferred wear especially during summertime. It has a natural lightness along with an inherent stiffness, which keeps the fabric from clinging to the skin. In spite of this lightness it is extremely strong, at least three times stronger than cotton. Linen has a breathable quality about it making it almost like a garment with miniature holes that keep the body well ventilated. Another quality that makes it popular for summer wear is its ability to absorb dampness. It keeps the body free from perspiration while at the same time drying quickly. Today, its exceptional capacity to resist static electric load makes it a preferred choice for use in space suits.

The beauty of any fabric increases because of its natural luster, and linen has this in large measures. The texture of the fabric depends upon the thickness of the yarns, but it is generally smooth which keeps it lint free. Like bamboo, regular washing makes it softer. The one drawback is a susceptibility to wrinkling, which calls for regular ironing to maintain the fabric's smooth feel. On the other hand, this wrinkled look is one of the factors that contribute to linen's unique charm. Consumers also enjoy the appeal of the *slubs* found on the fabric's face. Slubs, a defect of the fabric, are the small knots found scattered throughout linen, but as always, consumers embrace unique items different from the ordinary.

## Production

Linen is as much a product of its processing system as it is of its cultivation practices. Planting and harvesting methods play a vital role in determining the quality of the fiber and its organic nature. Linen qualifies as organic when it is grown in the absence of pesticides and toxic fertilizers. To ensure top-quality, long fibers while harvesting, the complete plant is pulled out of the ground, roots and all, or cut as close as possible to the roots. This also ensures retention of the natural color of the fiber.

The plant is then deseeded in a process called *rippling*, or even by *winnowing*. Being a bast fiber, the stalks are immersed in water in a process called retting. Retting disintegrates the *pectin*, which is there to hold the fibers together since almost 70% of the stem is cellulosic material. The next step in producing the fiber involves removal of the woody portion of the stem by crushing it between a set of rollers, and releasing the fibers in a process called *scutching*. The fibers are then combed with the *heckling comb*, which removes the short fibers (tow fibers) leaving behind the typically long, beautiful flax fibers (line fibers), which are used to create the finest garments and home accessories. Alternately, consumer products made with coarser linen fabric are made from the shorter tow fibers.

## Environmental Concerns

Organic linen is an environmentally friendly fiber mainly on account of its easy cultivation practices as well as natural processing methods. The soil does not need extra nutrients, eliminating the need for fertilizers. During the 14 to 15 weeks it takes the plant to mature, water provided by natural precipitation is generally enough for its growth. Although certain countries use expensive machines to harvest the stalk, pulling by hand is still the preferred method to ensure long fibers.

## Color/Dyeability

Naturally colored organic linen ranges from ivory to white and from tan to beige, and even gray, and gives a radiance that attracts without being overpowering. The dyeing methods for linen are varied, and as such, organic dyeing methods prevent negative environmental impact and are preferred for organic linen. However, non-reactive, earth-friendly dyes offer an alternative to these natural colors reaching any shade available on the market today.

## End Uses

All parts of the flax plant are useful. The seeds are used for cultivation as well as to prepare oil, varnish, pharmaceuticals, and cosmetics. The short, tow fibers are used for making blended fabrics, ropes, paper, non-wovens, and building composite material. The *shive*, or the broken stalk, is used to make chipboard panels, bedding for horses, and used as chaff which helps farmers to protect fruits and vegetables from coming in direct contact with soil.

Fabric uses are many ranging from fashionable clothing for men, women, and children to accessories for the home. As noted, linen is even applied in astronaut suiting. The traditional use of linen was in creating beautiful table wear, bed linen, upholstery, draperies, and wall coverings. Now, the pure, white linen shirt has become a must in both the male and female wardrobe. Its lightness makes it ideal for fashionable resort wear, and in places with high humidity and heat, it is ideal day wear.

## Care

Linen is very easy to care for, but due to its lack of elasticity it is important to shift the folds every time it is stored. Being folded in the same place tends to break the fiber over time leading to tears. It shows resistance to moths and beetles, but it is susceptible to damage from bleach, mildew, and perspiration. Dirt and stains can be easily removed by simple machine washing. Ironing the backside of the fabric ensures longevity and will help retain the natural luster.

## Organic Linen

Absorbs dampness
Susceptible to breakage
Cool, fresh and breathable in hot weather
Naturally colored, yet takes well to dyes
Shows lack of elasticity
Exceptional fabric preservation qualities
Very light, natural hand
Generally stays lint-free
Subtle luster and natural sheen
Grows without need for pesticides or fertilizers
Resistant to moths and beetles
Becomes softer with regular washing
Resists static electric load
Stiff quality to the finished fabric
Extremely strong, 3 times stronger than cotton
Susceptible to damage from bleach, mildew,
and perspiration
Sustainable resource, grows plentifully
Well ventilated, fabric has an air-like quality
Excellent moisture wicking abilities
High wrinkle propensity

## Characteristics

"Wool is a remarkable fiber - its thermal properties will keep us warm in the winter, reducing the need to turn up the heating, and keep us cool in the summer - as it does for the sheep themselves. It is versatile and durable. A wool garment can be treasured and worn for decades then when we return it to the earth it will quickly biodegrade without leaving a trace."

Isobel Davies, Green Fashion Designer
Izzy Lane Ltd | izzylane.com

# Guide to Green Fabrics™

Eco-friendly textiles for fashion and interior design

guidetogreenfabrics.com

Organic Wool

## Overview

Woollen pelts of ancient times paved the way for the sophisticated woollen clothing of modern times, which has ultimately led to the creation of organic woollen fiber in our green age. The use of conventional wool is slowly losing pace to organic wool in man's race to show himself as an ecologically sensitive creature. Organic wools are free from chemicals, such as pesticides, as they come from sheep which are not exposed to toxins. These sheep have been reared in absolutely healthy conditions, fit for both survival and for production of high quality wool.

Produced from healthy varieties of sheep raised on specialized organic farms, the wool produced is soft and comfortable. The best organic wool comes from Merino sheep which are organically raised. There are different standards in various countries with regard to organic certification. These standards are either set forth by the government or non-profit organizations. Sometimes even private companies play a deciding role in setting the standard. The Organic Trade Association (OTA), which represents the organic industry in North America, is the certifying body for organic wool.

## Region

Most organic wool comes from New Zealand and Australia, the prime producers of almost every kind of wool. Organic wool can also be sourced from England, the United States, Turkey, and Argentina, among other countries. Australia produces almost one-fourth of this kind of wool, while the United States is its largest consumer. According to a report from the OTA, 19,152 pounds of organic wool was harvested from sheep raised organically in the United States and Canada during the 2005 season. New Mexico led this effort with over 15,000 pounds alone.

## Properties

Organic wool is just as soft and comfortable as cotton. It dries quickly and adapts very fast to body temperature depending on atmospheric circumstances. It keeps one cool, or warm, depending on environmental conditions. It has hypo-allergenic and anti-bacterial properties which makes it more desirable than conventional wool. Organic wool absorbs perspiration and vapors, and is a self cleaning fiber which can last for years. However, it is more expensive to produce and procure than conventional wool, which is the only prohibitive factor that stands in the mass popularization of this eco-friendly product.

The *crimping* property of organic wool makes it naturally resilient and elastic, as the fiber bends and turns into a three-dimensional structure. This property makes the fiber durable, warm, and resistant to abrasion. This fiber can also absorb 30% of its weight in moisture which makes it suitable for all kinds of climates. Since wool retains moisture it resists flames, and upon burning, chars and extinguishes naturally. The durability of organic wool is such that it can be bent 20,000 times and not break. This elasticity makes it resistant to tearing. It can also be stretched up to 50% its original size in the dry state, and 30% in its wet state, and spring back to its original size upon release.

## Production

Wool is certified organic if it is produced in accordance with federal standards. For proper production it is imperative that the sheep or livestock used for procuring the raw material be bred organically. Organic breeding of livestock does not permit bathing sheep in chemicals to get rid of parasites. The use of chemicals like synthetic pesticides is completely prohibited, as is the use of genetic engineering or synthetic hormones. The animals should graze only on land which has proper natural grazing capacity. It is certified organic when the OTA is convinced that organic producers use the methods and materials allowed for its production. The breeds of sheep used for the production of organic wool are: Columbia, Navajo - Churro, Rambouillet, Suffolk Cross, Border Leicester, Cheviot, Cormo, Dorset, Karakul, Icelandic, Southdown, Suffolk, Tunis and unspecified crosses.

Organic wool is gathered by shearing the woolen fleece of the sheep. After shearing, the wool is separated into four categories: fleece, broken, bellies, and locks. This classifying of wool is known as *wool classing*. After shearing, the process of scouring takes place when grease, dirt, dead skin, sweat residue, and vegetable matter are removed from the wool. Production of organic wool is labor intensive and the wool is harvested annually.

## Environmental Concerns

Organic wool can be regarded as eco-friendly as it is produced without any harm being done to the animals or the environment. It is free from chemicals like pesticides and insecticides. Organic wool certification requires organic farming practices which are also friendly to humans working on the farms, so as not to expose them to harmful chemicals and pesticides.

## Color/Dyeability

Organic wool is generally creamy white in color but some sheep produce wool of natural colors like black, brown, silver, and random mixes. In order for it to retain its organic label, organic wool should be dyed using organic dyes only, as it accepts color naturally. These wools absorb dyes uniformly which allow it to achieve rich color. Low-impact, metal-free dye is also used on organic wool.

## End Uses

Organic wool can be substituted for ordinary wool. Its application is the same as of traditional wool. With every passing day it is finding new and varied uses. Some of the products for which organic wool is used are baby clothes, blankets, sweaters, socks, saddle cloth, and coats. Organic wool is widely used to cover heavy machinery. It is used in stereos and sound systems as it absorbs odor and noise. Organic Merino wool, which is the finest variety of organic wool, is used to make baby products like infant sleeping bags, baby wraps, and saddles. It is also used as fabric for underwear because it absorbs moisture and prevents heat and sweat rashes, which tend to harm baby's delicate skin.

men's wool suiting

Organic wool is just as soft and comfortable as cotton. It dries quickly and
adapts very fast to body temperature depending on atmospheric circumstances.
It keeps one cool, or warm, depending on environmental conditions.

U.S. federal regulations demand that mattresses are to be made of fire resistant material. Organic wool is a popluar choice for this product, as it also prevents bed bug infestation. It is an environmentally preferable material for carpets particularly when they are used with formaldehyde-free glue. Because of its flame resistance, wool carpets are specified in high risk, public environments like trains and airplanes.

## Care

A popular misconception among people is that maintenance of organic wool requires professional care. Taking care of organic wool is a relatively simple task. Washing should be done using a biodegradable detergent. This fabric does not take well to alkaline detergents. The water temperature should be mild. The preferred mode for washing is hand washing. Next, after removing an organic wool garment from the washing tub, gently shake it to remove excess water. The garment should be placed on a dry cotton towel and laid flat. This helps to remove moisture and odor. Organic wool should not be dried in direct sunlight as it may result in color fading. Once the garment is completely dry it should be folded flat and wrapped in a natural wrapper, but never in plastic.

## Organic Wool

Adapts to body temperature
Airy, breathable, dries easily
Anti-bacterial
100% biodegradable
Durable, abrasion resistant
Resists electricity
Fire retardant, extinguishes naturally
Hygroscopic, naturally absorbs moisture
Hypo-allergenic
Chemical, toxin, and pesticide-free
Naturally resilient and elastic, has natural crimp
Retains heat, keeps you warm
Soft and comfortable
Resistant to tearing

## Characteristics

sun ripened pineapples

Piña fabric made in the Philippines is the finest example of this material and its diaphanous, gossamer like quality makes it a much coveted item. Limited availability of the fabric has made it an expensive product and most connoisseurs of the fabric belong to the wealthy sections of society.

"Increasing awareness on various environmental problems has led to a shift in the way consumers go about their lives. There has been a change in consumer attitudes towards green products. People are actively trying to reduce their impact on the environment by buying green products. However, this is not widespread enough and is still evolving."

Namita Rautray, Eco-Manufacturer
Inovex Enterprises PVT. LTD. | inovexenterprises.com

# Guide to Green Fabrics™

### Eco-friendly textiles for fashion and interior design

guidetogreenfabrics.com

Pina

## Overview

By opening employment avenues, the fabric made from the piña, or the pineapple palm plant, has brought economic independence and prosperity to the natives of the Philippines and other countries. Women are as much in demand for their dexterity in weaving this diaphanous, delicate fiber as they are for the aesthetic value they bring to the fabric through embroidery. Like most green fibers it commands a premium in the marketplace due to its labor intensive methods of production and cultivation. Its elegance and exquisite drapery make it a much sought after fabric to be used for special occasions, and it is frequently bequeathed as an heirloom to one's special child. The name is derived from the literal Spanish word *piña*, meaning pineapple.

Pineapple is a tropical plant that grows best in places with moderate to extreme climates and on low elevations. Pineapples abhor cold and extremes of cold can retard growth of the plant. Elevation at which the plant is cultivated impacts the sweetness and acidity of the fruit, although in fiber extraction this does not matter. As a nod to its durability, pineapple will also grow in places with low rainfall.

## Region

Pineapple is widely cultivated in the Philippines, Hawaii, India, West Indies, Indonesia, South America, East Asia, Sri Lanka, Africa, and Australia. Production routinely takes place in local communities, which export to other countries.

## Properties

The leaves produce a silky fiber, which is delicate yet very strong, sometimes even stiff, and white or ivory in color. The fiber is as thin as hair, soft and fine, and is naturally lustrous. Almost see-through, piña is lightweight and has an elegant and beautiful appearance. It has an excellent textural quality that gives it character. It is naturally saltwater resistant and does not easily wear down. Expensive, heirloom-like wedding garments are fashioned from this fiber, which is often blended with silk or polyester. It appears and behaves similar to linen, yet is softer than hemp. Because of its scarcity and hand management techniques, it is considered rare and is very expensive.

## Production

Certain species of pineapple are grown for the explicit purpose of producing fiber. In such plants, the fruit is cut off in its initial stages so as to allow for greater fiber output. Piña fiber is extracted from the leaves by hand scraping with instruments fashioned out of coconut shells and sometimes even bits of broken pottery. In Sri Lanka, bamboo is used to expose the epidermis, which leaves the fiber revealed for extraction. To create a *filament* effect, the fibers are knotted at the ends with one another, after which they are transferred to a spinning wheel. The process of weaving is carried out on hand looms operated manually. The fibers are painstakingly inserted into the reeds, owing to their fragility. It is a time consuming process that takes up to a day and a half to accomplish. Once the fibers have been woven into fabric, it is pounded so as to allow the knots to seamlessly merge. Weaving a fabric without knots is almost impossible as the fibers are extremely susceptible to breakage.

## Environmental Concerns

Advances in fabric production have greatly altered the way cloth is made, but in the case of piña, the manufacturing process remains the same as it was 100 years ago. Being a by-product of a plant used mainly for edible purposes, piña wears the badge of being environmentally friendly for its purposed mission. No part of production involves gas emissions, excessive exhaust, runoff, or degradation to agriculture or animal life. Its green qualities are also derived from the fact that it does not use electrical, chemical, or mechanical inputs in its production. It is indeed a major player in energy conservation in the world of textiles.

## Color/Dyeability

Piña is utilized in its natural shades that range from a pure white to lustrous ivory, and hence, the dyeing process is largely eliminated. However, piña takes especially well to vegetable dyes including from leaves, fruit, and tree bark. It is blended with cotton, silk, and abaca to create exquisite textured fabrics. It retails as piña–seda, or piña silk, when blended with silk, and is less expensive than pure piña. It combines in itself the qualities of various fibers, being comparatively better in texture than silk, in softness better than hemp, and in appearance similar to linen.

## End Uses

Piña fabric made in the Philippines is the finest example of this material and its diaphanous, gossamer-like quality makes it a much coveted item. Limited availability of the fabric has made it an expensive product and most connoisseurs of the fabric belong to the wealthy sections of society. In the Philippines, the *Barong Tagalong*, which are formal dresses and wedding dresses, are the most recognized items made from piña. The hand embroidery applied to garments made of piña, called piña calado, place the items at the top of any fashion wish list. The people of the Haiman Island in China have fabricated a coarse variety of the material, which looks similar to grass cloth. Indian shoemakers use piña thread in their manufacturing process while West Africans are known to use it for making caps and capes as well as a stringing material for jewelry. In Guam, fishermen use it to make their nets and also for wrapping cigars. Mats, bags, linens, and table fashions are made of piña. The fibers are also used for making ropes, twine, and paper.

## Care

A fabric with such extraordinary qualities needs tender loving care and piña demands the gentlest variety. Dry cleaning and machine washing of these fabrics is strictly prohibited. The best way to wash piña fabric is by soaking it in a mild detergent and washing the garment by hand. In case of yellowing it can be soaked in vinegar-water overnight and then washed in soapy water. The cloth should not be wrung or twisted, and the best rinsing motion is an up-down motion followed by drip-drying. After the excess water drains off, the garment should be laid flat to dry. Ironing the slightly damp garment gives best results.

## Pina

100% biodegradable
Naturally white or ivory in color
Delicate yet very strong
Does not take to dry cleaning
Durable, does not easily wear
Can be dyed with vegetable dyes
Avoids electrical, chemical, or mechanical inputs
Lightweight with elegant, beautiful appearance
Naturally lustrous
Considered rare and very expensive
Salt water resistant
Offers silky, soft, fine fibers
Softer than hemp
Has excellent textural qualities
Thin as strands of hair, or finer
Best washed by hand

## Characteristics

"Home and occupant health can be improved by having textiles that are organically grown and milled without chemicals. These textiles make for better, cleaner indoor air quality, potentially reducing allergies. There is also the satisfaction of supporting sustainable farming."

Sarah Barnard, Green Interior Designer
Sarah Barnard Design | sarahbarnarddesign.blogspot.com

# Guide to Green Fabrics™

Eco-friendly textiles for fashion and interior design

guidetogreenfabrics.com

Ramie

## Overview/ Region

A fabric that in lightness can be compared to the wings of a dragonfly is a similarity that one can use to describe ramie (*Boehmeria nivea*), an ancient fiber crop in use by humanity for the past 6,000 years. It derives from the nettle plant family Urticaceae. The Chinese absolutely prize ramie, and in times past, garments made of this translucent fabric were brought out of treasure chests to celebrate the onset of summer. A specific day, the 5th day of the 5th lunar month according to the Chinese calendar, was set out for festivities. Young women would deck themselves in their finest ramie clothes and cavort, unbridled by the bulk of their winter garments. Chinese emperors were presented with gifts of ramie as a mark of respect and gratitude. Accordingly, the effort put into the weaving is so great and time-consuming that a gift of such distinction speaks volumes about the giver and the receiver. The world's leading ramie cultivators include China, East Asia, India, Philippines, Brazil, Thailand, Malay Peninsula, Taiwan, and South Korea. The leading producer is China, and France, Germany, the United Kingdom, and Japan are fortunate to be countries to which China's prized ramie is exported. The international supply is limited, therefore, ramie's utilization takes place mostly domestically.

## Properties

A fiber of Chinese origin, ramie has been found in the tombs of the Pharaohs of Egypt, testifying to the special status of the fabric that comes from its innate mold and bacteria resistant qualities. It also has excellent absorption abilities as well as quick drying features, making it suitable for tropical and humid weather. Ramie is one of the strongest natural fibers known to man, and when wet, its strength increases manifold. It is much stronger than linen and cotton. Ramie fabrics have the quality of being able to hold their shape while avoiding wrinkles. Because of its high molecular crystallinity, ramie is more brittle and less durable than other natural fibers. Therefore, it is blended with various fibers so as to enhance its strength while imparting a silky texture to the blend. Ramie shows good absorption and density, but when it comes to resilience, elasticity, and elongation, it is found lacking. It's for these reasons that the fabric tends to be brittle and also breaks and tears if it is repeatedly folded at the same point. The fibers are also extremely fine. Woven in the Hansan province of China, ramie is so fine that a rice bowl can hold an entire bolt of the fabric.

## Production

Ramie is a bast fiber whose stalk contains the fibrous part and the harvesting is done either before or after the plant begins to flower. This is the best suited time for maximum fiber extraction with the stem of the plant being cut close to the lateral root. Harvesting is also done by bending the stem of the plant so as to break the core and extract the cortex from the point of origin. Decortication is done while the plants are still fresh, since drying tends to make fiber extraction extremely difficult. The ribbons of fiber thus extracted are allowed to dry naturally and speedily. Unlike other bast fibers, this fiber has to be chemically processed to remove the gum, which is present in the stem. Ramie produces a naturally white fiber which does not require bleaching, adding another positive factor to its environmentally friendly qualifications. Due to its brittle nature, ramie weaving is done in humid conditions to prevent thread breakage. In olden days, weaving was done in underground basements that would hold moisture, and water was kept handy to sprinkle on the fiber in case the fabric became dry. In modern establishments, this job is accomplished by humidifier.

The fabric is soaked in water and dried in the sun, a process repeated several times in order to obtain a sparkling white color. Ramie is a relatively expensive product due to the various, laborious steps needed in its extraction and manufacture. As one can imagine, spinning is also a tough job due to ramie's brittle quality.

## Environmental Concerns

The environmentally friendly attributes of the fiber derive from the fact that it is a hardy perennial plant and can be harvested as many as six times annually, therefore qualifying it as sustainable agriculture. The plant has a lifespan anywhere between 6 and 20 years, depending upon cultivation and harvesting techniques. Ramie fibers take well to natural dyes, including vegetable dyes, in a wide variety of colors. Fiber-reactive dyes are also used to produce colorfast ramie fabrics in all hues.

## End Uses

Ramie is put to a number of excellent uses, the chief applications being in the manufacture of fishing nets, filter cloths, packing materials, and industrial grade sewing thread. It is blended with wool and cotton to create both clothing as well as household furnishings such as canvas and upholstery. However, textile use can be limited because of ramie's brittleness as well as the presence of uneven fibers. Paper manufactured with shorter ramie fibers also finds its way into retail. Recently, automotive giant Toyota™ began integrating new ecological bioplastics made of plant cellulose into Prius™ models in an effort to reduce petroleum use. Ramie is one of the principal crops being used for this effort.

## Care

Ramie needs to be stored extremely carefully due to its brittle quality, but laundering and washing does not require the same amount of care since the fabric takes on additional strength when it is wet. It is best to hand wash ramie in cool water, then lay garments or items flat to dry. With each wash, the fabric becomes more lustrous and smooth. Items will hold their shape and not shrink. The fabric can also tolerate high temperatures.

## Ramie

Anti-bacterial
Quite brittle, less durable fabric
Naturally white in color
Dries quickly, avoids wrinkles
Takes well to natural and fiber-reactive dyes
Relatively expensive product
Harvested as many as 6 times annually
Has light, translucent, fine qualities
Becomes more lustrous and smooth
through washings
Lacks resilience, elasticity, and elongation
Mold and mildew resistant
Has silky texture when blended
One of the strongest natural fibers
Qualifies as sustainable agriculture
Tears if repeatedly folded in same place
Becomes stronger when wet

## Characteristics

"There are benefits at different life-cycle stages of the organic and eco-friendly fabrics trade, both for consumers and producers. As the demand for such eco-friendly items is increasing, there exists a great scope for new entrepreneurs to enter into this field."

Namita Rautray, Eco-Manufacturer
Inovex Enterprises PVT. LTD. | inovexenterprises.com

# Guide to Green Fabrics™

Eco-friendly textiles for fashion and interior design

guidetogreenfabrics.com

## Recycled Nylon

# Overview

Images of landfills bulging with discarded plastic bottles, waste cuttings from industrial products, and *pre-consumer waste* has become a part of our global landscape. Recycled nylon uses waste that would otherwise have taken decades to decompose and converts it into beautiful, green fiber.

Today, chic swimwear, exercise apparel, and smart jackets that hang in the finest department stores are created from recycled material. Huge volumes of nylon and other scrap material continue to grow with the manufacture of products that ever more depend on nylon for their primary needs. There is also pre-consumer waste generated during production. The use of these waste materials provides the resources needed to manufacture recycled nylon.

The ubiquitous office carpet, whose primary function is to be durable, is one of the most widespread applications of recycled nylon. It provides the raw material needed to produce it again, upon discarding it after much wear and tear. With even a fraction of the 250 million pounds being recycled annually, it creates a huge volume of recycled nylon.

## Region

Recycled nylon is not an agricultural fiber, and as such, its production is dependent upon the areas where newer technologies that can convert waste into nylon fiber are found. Its production is also centered in areas where significant industrial and *post-consumer waste* are generated. On that basis, China and the United States of America are the two nations that have seen primacy in its production.

## Properties

The fiber has adequate bulk, crimp, and texture which gives it an elegant and shiny look. Being a synthetic fiber, it is inherently resistant to bacteria and microbes and is resistant to mold. The synthetic nature of the fabric also makes it resistant to pilling. It is easy to dye recycled nylon in all shades according to personal or commercial tastes and needs.

## Production

Because there are many different types of nylon produced, recyclers must wade through discards to be sure they capture the correct types for processing. Nylon 6 bears quite a lot of this attention, and other nylons must be properly matched so that recycling efforts line up. The production of recycled nylon begins with accumulating available pre and *post-industrial waste*, and then converting it into chips, which are melted into polymer. To make these chips, the raw material is chopped, ground, and melted, and then put through a conversion process, which creates nylon chips through reformulation of the material. It is these chips that are turned into filaments using a proprietary process unique to individual companies, although they follow a basic procedure to create the polymer. This polymer is then extruded through spinnerets. The resultant filament is combined together to make strong yarn, which is processed in a way that allows it to acquire bulk, strength, and crimp. The process of texturing is what gives the fabric its elasticity, comfort, and softness.

## Environmental Concerns

Virgin nylon used for clothing, accessories, car components, furnishings, and carpet uses crude oil. The process of converting crude into fiber is a manifold process, where the energy and chemicals used in its production impact the environment in negative ways. With recycled nylon, benefits to the environment are doubled, for not only does waste become utilized productively, but stress upon the land is also reduced. By recycling products, industries can affirm their commitment to the environment without hurting their bottom lines. Recycled nylon is especially environmentally friendly in relation to virgin polyester because it eliminates some of the most environmentally degrading practices of making polyester. The entire process of converting crude oil into virgin polyester is eliminated with only polymerization, extrusion, and texturing as the energy consuming parts of the operation.

The biggest environmental benefit of recycled nylon is that it reduces stress on finite crude oil resources that are already stretched to the breaking point. Since it is made from previously processed material, the amount of carbon released in its production is substantially lesser relative to virgin nylon. In its use of discards, it once again reiterates its green properties, which are further enhanced by the fact that recycled nylon is once again recyclable. When post-consumer items are used innovatively to create new products, the need for creating new landfills can be minimized. As noted, landfills harm the environment through leaching of chemicals into the earth and release of noxious fumes, including *methane gas*, into the atmosphere during the process of decay and decomposition. Thus, available land can ideally be used for more constructive purposes.

## End Uses

While apparel holds the most important use of recycled nylon with American, British, Chinese, and Japanese designers using it to design sports wear, the use of recycled nylon in carpet making is also very great. Offices use huge amounts of carpet as floor covering to give interiors an elegant look. Carpets made from recycled nylon, which is used as pile yarn, are not only economical, but also eco-friendly. The above-mentioned are just a couple of uses of this multifaceted fiber whose application ranges from clothing to packaging. Recycled nylon is extensively used in the creation of performance clothing as well as uniforms, working apparel, socks, dress pants, and innerwear such as vests. In the furnishings industry it is used to cater to the demands of the hotel industry as well as hospitals. While the former uses recycled nylon to give itself the tag of "green hotel" by using it for drapes and bed sheets, the latter uses it for making furniture and privacy curtains. It is also used to make sewing thread, zipper tapes, product labels, tote bags, office paneling, and seating, as well as banners and signboards.

## Recycled Nylon

Has anti-wrinkle properties
Inherently resistant to bacteria,
mold, and microbes
High strength and durability,
good sound conductor
Easy care fabric, does not shrink
Has elasticity, comfort and softness
Elegant, shiny appearance
Fewer energy outputs than virgin nylon
Pill-free fabric
Has adequate bulk, crimp, and texture

## Characteristics

"We need more farmers willing to grow organic and sustainable crops. It's quite a complex operation and not so simple to change. It would benefit the environment if harmful and toxic practices were not used to manufacture what we wear."

Deborah Lindquist, Green Fashion Designer
Deborah Lindquist Eco Fashion Brand | deborahlindquist.com

# Guide to Green Fabrics™

Eco-friendly textiles for fashion and interior design

guidetogreenfabrics.com

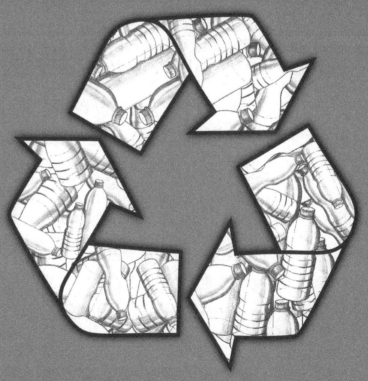

Recycled Polyester

## Overview

In an effort to introduce closed-loop thinking to everyday consumers, recycled polyester manufacturers are fashioning reuse concepts in new and significant ways. Through support of eco-friendly practices in the development of products made for them, consumers can share in this eco-success, particularly with recycled polyester. The process of using existing, traditional polyester (polyethylene terephthalate (PET)) to develop recycled polyester can enlighten and engage consumers and help them lower our global carbon footprint. The key is to make aware the fact that breaking down polyester fabric to its molecular structure and reproducing it can be an environmental plus in many ways, and that the technology is readily available today. However, all aspects of the lifecycle as well as the chemical composition of the fabric must be considered for a truly green experience. As evidenced, traditional polyester is a worldwide phenomenon with lasting power. Its easy care properties make it hard to beat in many ways, thus the efforts to recycle it are in line with consumer buying patterns because virgin polyester is likely to be produced for a very long time.

## Properties

Some of the advantages of using this fiber comes from its synthetic nature which discourages growth of bacteria and microbes leading to a mold and mildew free fabric, even when wet. Its anti-wrinkle nature does not exhibit any shrinkage, and it has high strength and durability. Being a filament yarn, protruding ends are eliminated leading to lint-free and pill-free fabrics.

## Environmental Concerns

Regarding its green standing, there are two important factors involved with the determination of recycled polyester's eco-label: its original material and the employed recycling methods. Traditional polyester is made with petroleum products and does not fall into the natural or sustainable fiber categories. Therefore, it is inherently chemically intensive, and this situation can present complications when breaking down and attempting to match fibers for recycling. The process must also be strictly contained because of the potential for harm to the environment through mishandling of liquid, petroleum-based chemicals. The potential for human health hazards must also be of constant care and concern.

Unlike EcoFi®, which uses plastic bottles to make new polyester, recycled polyester is born of broken down polyester fabric that is brought to life again and made into new polyester. It is simply a recycled version, and an environmentally friendly product with far reach, depending on its composition and methods. The raw materials used for making recycled polyester are abundantly available, and by using discarded materials, the recycling of these fibers aids in protecting the environment, which benefits the *ecosystem*. In addition, manufacturing recycled polyester reduces waste production and petroleum consumption. During this process, it is possible to reduce both energy consumption and carbon emissions by approximately 80% as compared to the process of producing raw polyester from petroleum.

Facts indicate that the estimation of the amount of barrels of oil it takes to produce traditional, virgin polyester is quite staggering at 70 million annually. An additional 34 million barrels are used for the production of plastic bottles. Only a fraction of these plastic bottles are used in the production of EcoFi®. With polyester being produced all over the world, it's hard to escape the reality of landfill overload from discarded garments.

recycled polyester fabric

Recycled polyester, an extremely low maintenance fabric, has many
uses for fashion, home interiors, and contract design. Fabric care is the
same as with traditional polyester, being easily machine washed and dried.

With respect to the actual process of recycling traditional polyester garments, the chemical composition and nature of the fibers is a concern, and hence, additional complexities abound, for example, with *antimony*. A toxic chemical compound that is similar to compounds found in arsenic, antimony is converted to antimony trioxide when it reaches high temperatures. The recycling process releases all of the fabric's compounds, including *carcinogens*, therefore allowing them to be taken in by humans, animals, and the land. This can cause breathing and respiratory problems including emphysema and other concerns. Further, toxic wastewater is the result of antimony trioxide being washed into it, and possibly into waterways.

Clearly, recycling polyester is a process that demands the strictest of controls, and another aspect of this process bears the realization that the fibers can only be recycled so many times until they are no longer strong enough to be useful. Environmental pioneer William McDonough termed this "downcycling" because of the breakdown of the fibers over time due to repeat recycling. As a boost to the improvement of certain associated dilemmas, an innovative fiber called Eco Intelligent® Polyester (EIP) was developed by a North American-based company, the Victor Group™. An antimony-free polyester with Cradle to Cradle™ Gold standing issued by McDonough Braungart Design Chemistry, this fiber resonates true closed-loop philosophy and methods alike.

It is the first "technical nutrient" textile that carries materials through the manufacturing system, into reuse, and throughout the recycling process without breaking down. This means the fiber can be refashioned into numerous products with no change in chemical composition. Eco Intelligent® Polyester also uses fully optimized dyes and chemicals, no chlorine, and is free of persistent bioaccumulative and toxic chemicals (PBTs).

Patagonia™, an American outdoor clothing manufacturer with leadership in the recycled polyester arena, uses recycling bins to collect worn-out clothing in its retail stores around the world. The used garments are recycled and reborn as new products. This is accomplished using their patented technology, ECO CIRCLE™, a closed-loop polyester recycling system introduced by the Teijin Group™. This technology enables discarded products to be repeatedly recycled without compromising quality because they are chemically decomposed to the molecular level, and then purified to form raw materials of the same quality as those made from petroleum. Since the system was launched in 2002, more than 100 companies worldwide, consisting of mostly apparel and sportswear manufacturers, have utilized ECO CIRCLE™. The number of members continues to increase including major, global manufacturers.

## End Uses/ Care

Recycled polyester, an extremely low maintenance fabric, has many uses for fashion, home interiors, and contract design. Fabric care is the same as with traditional polyester, being easily machine washed and dried. However, there are also benefits from air drying without wrinkling that the fiber takes to quite well. Collective dedication to recycling is part of what moves us closer to a greener planet, including marked efforts to make the public aware of their role in the recycled polyester process. As long as awareness of the production intricacies is present, consumers can make informed decisions about recycled polyester as a fabric choice.

# Recycled Polyester

Has anti-wrinkle properties
Curbs waste production and
petroleum consumption
Discourages growth of bacteria and microbes
Has high strength and durability
Lint-free, pill-free
Extremely low maintenance
Stays mold and mildew-free
Reduces energy consumption and
carbon emissions by 80%
Creates less air, water, and soil contamination

# Characteristics

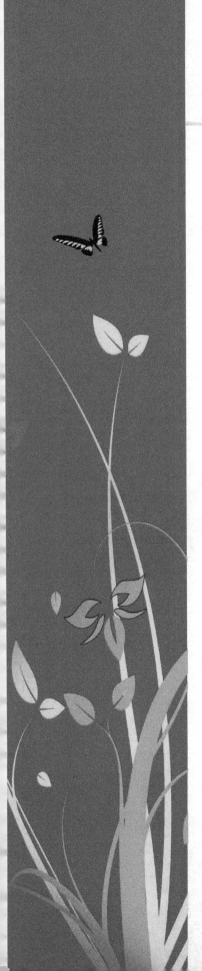

# Designer Spotlight

## Namita Rautray

As a senior executive and brand ambassador to India-based Inovex Enterprises Pvt. Ltd., Namita Rautray has been an inspiration to women throughout India as well as to up and coming eco-designers on the global design scene. Her product, Safix™ Scrub Pad, available in Canada, UAE, Hong Kong, India, and Australia is made from 100% non-woven coconut fiber (coir) bound together by a non-toxic adhesive, which can be used for all-purpose household cleaning. Her company's invention is based on the basic foundation to provide an effective, cost efficient, and environmentally safe scouring pad which will not leave toxic residues in landfills. She explains, "Hazardous wastes are poisonous byproducts of manufacturing, farming, city septic systems, construction, automotive garages, laboratories, hospitals, and other industries. The waste may be liquid, solid, or sludge and contain chemicals, heavy metals, radiation, dangerous pathogens, or other toxins. Even households generate hazardous waste from items such as cleaning detergents and scouring pads necessary for cleaning. Often, this waste is dangerous to both nature and human life and the levels of dangerous wastes continue to grow." Namita says that after spending years near a coastal belt in India surrounded by coconut plantations she had an opportunity to discover coir, which she calls "a gift of nature." After extensive research the invention was born – a scrub pad made from white coir fibers, which have a natural gift of abrasive texture. She goes on to describe the lives of women in rural India, which, according to her, continue to be grimed, with very little access to education or healthcare. Her brand strives to employ and engage these women. "A simple skill required for sorting loose coir fiber is a vital step for manufacturing a scrub pad that has transformed the lives of rural women in India," she states. Inovex Enterprises Pvt. Ltd. believes in the theory of reciprocity, which means that since the company's product is targeted at women consumers its social endeavors should focus directly on the economic empowerment of women. In summary, Namita states, "Maintaining ecological balance is a major issue confronting the corporate world today. The damage done to the environment has already crossed the threshold and reached alarming limits. All these negative developments have forced mankind to think more seriously about conserving the environment."

Inovex Enterprises Pvt. Ltd. | inovexenterprises.com

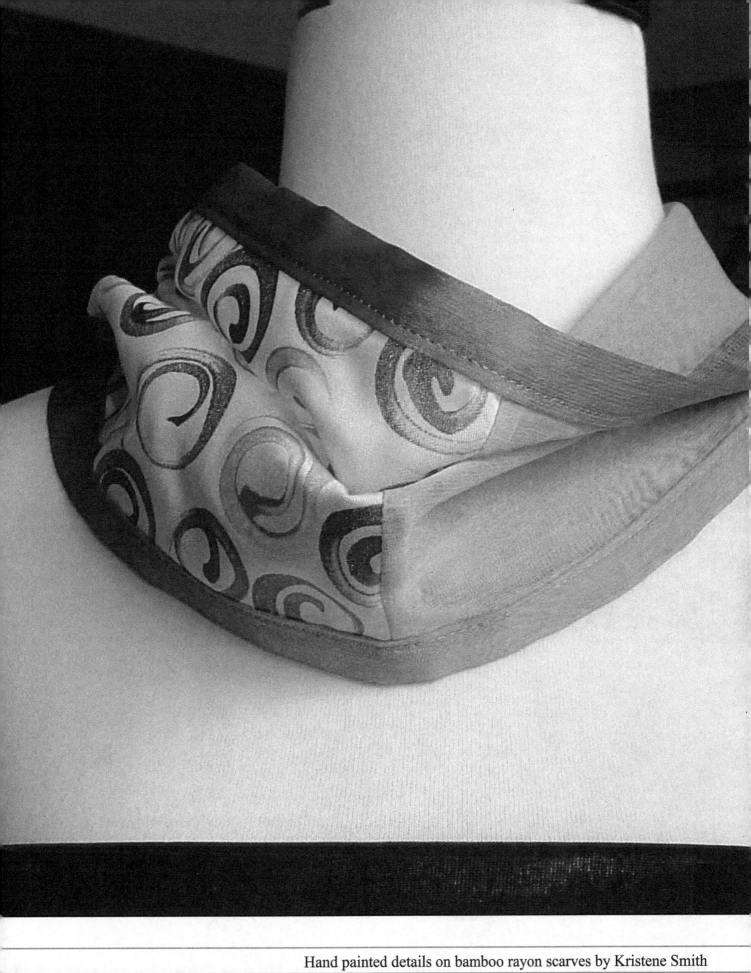

Hand painted details on bamboo rayon scarves by Kristene Smith

recycled wool suiting

It is the crimp, or the inherent waviness of wool, that allows for
air retention and bulk in the fiber, endowing it with insulation.
The most amazing quality of its insulation is the ability to trap
heat in cold climates and to keep the heat out in warmer places.

"Eco friendly fabrics are fantastic to work with. Widely available in textures and solids, prints are sometimes harder to come by. However, what is not easily sourced in natural fabrics can often be found in recycled, non-toxic options that are still better for the environment."

Sarah Barnard, Green Interior Designer
Sarah Barnard Design | sarahbarnarddesign.blogspot.com

# Guide to Green Fabrics™

## Eco-friendly textiles for fashion and interior design

guidetogreenfabrics.com

Recycled Wool

## Overview

One of the greenest fibers available today is recycled wool, or wool that is reused after having outlived its original application. Thus, recycled wool has all the properties of virgin wool, but instead of filling up landfills or lying idle in cupboards, this is wool that has discovered a way of being useful yet again. In order to study the properties, manufacture, processing, dyeing, and the sources of recycled wool, a general study of wool is the starting point. The use of wool by human beings to make warm clothes has been around since the time people learned to domesticate animals, especially sheep. Wool is a fiber that is produced by the follicles of certain members of the Caprinae family, to which sheep belong. Goats, llamas and rabbits also provide humans with wool, but not of the same quality as found in the sheep family. Sheep's wool is set apart from the hairy fibers taken from other animals by the ease with which it can be spun. The ease in spinning results from the scaling and *crimp* of the wool, which allows for easy attachment of one fiber to another. It is the crimp, or the inherent waviness of wool, that allows for air retention and bulk in the fiber, endowing it with insulation. The most amazing quality of its insulation is the ability to trap heat in cold climates and to keep the heat out in warmer places. This makes it the preferred choice for the nomads of the desert, the Bedouins. Long ago, wool garments were very much in demand and many towns and countries in Europe had a flourishing trade in wool manufacture. Before silk became the mainstay of Italian trade, it was wool that had been filling up the coffers of the legendary Medici family. The importance of wool as an item of trade can be understood from the numerous laws the British made in order to prevent smuggling of wool, an activity which was termed *owling*.

The quality of wool is dependent upon many factors, and varieties which combine these in the greatest and best proportion are termed "finest." After shearing the sheep, the fiber has to be of a specific length, which is called *staple length*. The diameter of the wool, although only in microns, is an important attribute in judging the quality of the fiber. The feel of the fiber against the skin, whether it is soft or rough, is termed *hand*, while the wavy texture of the wool is called the crimp. The natural shine or glow of the fiber, or the *luster*, is an important factor in determining the quality of the wool as are the array of natural colors.

## Region

Australia and New Zealand lead world production of wool, while it is also produced in significant amounts in China, Iran, the United Kingdom, Turkey, India, Sudan, South Africa, and Argentina. The finest quality of wool available is sourced from Merino sheep of Australia, while sheep from New Zealand provide crossbreed wool.

## Properties

Apart from the unique, natural, and extreme insulation properties that wool has, it is also *hygroscopic*, meaning it absorbs moisture. At the same time, it is *hydrophobic*, meaning the exterior of the fiber repels water, therefore keeping one dry. Its rate of combustion is very low, as is its flammability tendency. It offers low amounts of heat release, which makes it ideal for application in those spheres that call for good combustion protection. It is for this reason that carpet made of wool is used in trains and airplanes so as to reduce the danger of spread of fire in case of accidents and other eventualities. The protective gear worn by firemen, and often soldiers, sometimes has a wool component in it.

## Production

The process of turning wool from raw material into fiber begins after the wool has been sheared off the sheep's body. The wool at this stage contains several impurities like dirt, dust, sweaty residues, and dead skin, but also *lanolin*, a valued product. The sheared wool at this stage is called *greased wool* or *wool in the grease*. This greased wool is cleaned thoroughly by *scouring*, and in preparing wool for commercial uses, it is sometimes put through a process called *carbonization* to remove vegetable matter. At this stage, fibers can be made into yarns and knitted or woven into wool fabric. The leftover lanolin is used in the cosmetics industry.

## Environmental Concerns

After having outlived its utility and fascination for the owners, wool garments, items, and accessories are normally discarded. The discarded goods, when put to multiple uses in lieu of fresh wool, constitute the segment of recycled woolen products. Recycled wool is one of the greenest of all natural fibers because it is being reused without any additional expenditure and is a revenue earner with least investment, both ecological and financial. Because of savings on energy intensive processes in production and transportation, these fibers prove to be cheap both in sourcing and treatment. Usage of water is minimal since the wool does not have to be scoured, bleached, or dyed. As an animal protein fiber, the wool can be returned to the earth as soil fertilizer, slowly releasing essential amino acids and nitrogen.

## Color/Dyeability

The advances in technology in the field of dyeing allow for wool to be dyed in all possible shades. The best way of dyeing wool fibers is by using the reactive method that allows for the application of a range of colors with full penetration.

## End Uses

Coarse wool is used for making carpet, rugs, and other furnishing items while the finest wool is reserved for use in high-end garments often to enhance the male wardrobe, such as business suits. However, there are countless garments for women that boast expensive and expertly crafted features made from the finest wool in the world. Apart from these applications, recycled wool also finds extensive use in the manufacture of cover for cloth diapers. Innovative uses of recycled wool for everything from craft items to blankets, sweaters, and children's wear has caught on. This is one of those fashion trends that bodes well for the planet.

## Care

Garments made of recycled wool need tender care, and knowing the right way of caring for one's garment is as much an investment as is the actual purchase. Being a relatively weak fiber, it is best to use mild soaps and detergents and prevent soaking woolen garments for a long time. Wringing and pulling wool garments can lead to yarn breakage since the basic nature of wool is weak. After washing, wool garments should be lifted out of the water, the excess water squeezed out lightly, and the garment laid on a thick towel on a flat surface to absorb excess water. Wool takes a longer time to dry, so the garment should be left undisturbed, except for turning it over a couple of times to allow both sides to dry.

To keep wool garments safe from mildew and mold attacks, they should be aired often and allowed to dry in sunlight, which will rid the fiber of extra moisture, which is the breeding ground of these organisms. Because of its natural sulfur content, moths are attracted to wool. Protection from moths and their larvae should be done by placing cedar blocks, moth balls, or herbal sachets near garments.

## Recycled Wool

Characteristics

Low combustion rate
Cool in spring-like weather
Has natural crimp
Durable and sturdy
Low flammability tendency
Hydrophobic, repels water
Hygroscopic, absorbs moisture
Very insulating and warm
Seen as an investment in
one's wardrobe
High luster
Does not pill

"I was raised on a small farm and nature and wildlife were always very important to me. When I began my career in the fashion industry, I realized quickly that there is an entirely dark side of the apparel industry that the consumer does not see. It was my own experiences and lots of research that led me to want to produce in a completely different way."

Beth Doane, Green Fashion Designer
RainTees | raintees.com

# Guide to Green Fabrics™

## Eco-friendly textiles for fashion and interior design

guidetogreenfabrics.com

## Rush

Rush, also known as "fiber rush," is sourced from the different kinds of rushes, or weeds, that grow around swamps and wetlands. Soft rushes are found on almost all continents except Africa, and are used especially by the Japanese to make *tatami*, or floor mats. Rushes have hollow stems, making all items fabricated from it lightweight, including baskets and mats. Its natural color ranges from green to brown.

Cattail is one of the popular rush fibers used to fabricate chair seats. Rush should be gathered when the leaves are green, or only when the tips of the leaves and stalks are beginning to turn brown. This period corresponds to late July through early September. After having selected leaves that have a perfect shape, they should be allowed to dry for two to three weeks.

The drying process should be undertaken in dark, airy rooms after making bundles of similarly sized leaves. This is done so as to avoid excess sunlight, which may make the leaves brittle. Rush should always be dampened with water, as wetting makes the leaves pliable and easy to work with because dry rush tends to break easily. The resultant, woven products are quite stunning in visual quality and are imported and exported worldwide.

"The fashion industry needs an internal revolution to adopt a philosophy of respect and sustainability. It shouldn't be a reflection of the ills of today but a reflection of how things should be tomorrow."

Isobel Davies, Green Fashion Designer
Izzy Lane Ltd | izzylane.com

# Guide to Green Fabrics™

Eco-friendly textiles for fashion and interior design

guidetogreenfabrics.com

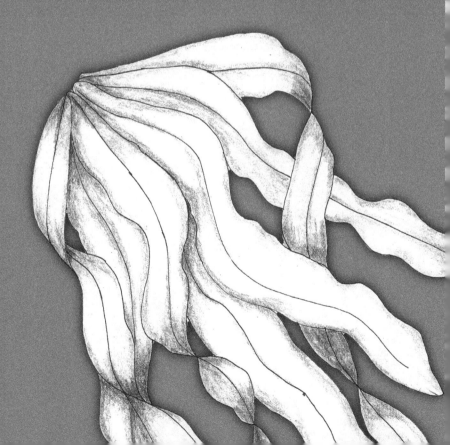

Sea Cell

The unfathomable depths of the seas and oceans hide within them unknown treasures, and one among these is found in seaweed, which can be transformed into fibers for making fabrics using modern technology. Seas and oceans abound with seaweed, which is a naturally occurring renewable resource. Seaweed fibers cannot stand on their own, and so a cellulose-based fabric is created using the lyocell process and it is this fabric which serves as the basis for sea cell fabric, commercially known as "seaweed." This organic, eco-friendly material captures the manifold advantages of natural fibers, but without causing any negative impact upon the environment.

Seaweed is full of nutrients and by transforming seaweed into fabric humans are able to partake of these nutrients, which nourish the skin. Moisture released by the body facilitates the absorption of calcium, magnesium, vitamins, and amino acids, which occur naturally in seaweed. It also protects the skin and has natural anti-inflammatory properties, which makes sea cell fabric blends somewhat hypo-allergenic. These properties also allow for the manufacture of garments and household accessories that are soft and breathable. These fabrics aid in skin cell regeneration and allow blood flow to the skin. Sea cell has anti-microbial properties, which makes it odor-free. It is mainly used to manufacture items where hygiene is at a premium, such as undergarments, personal hygiene products, and household products including bed sheets, towels, and carpets.

The beneficial use of seaweed has been known to man for centuries. Different cultures use it for different purposes. While the Japanese and Chinese prize seaweed for its therapeutic and curative properties, people in Britain and Ireland have been known to value seaweed as a nutrient rich food, and it is used as a dietary supplement. In a world full of stress, seaweed is prized as a food which can help combat stress and also aids in the detoxification of the body. The cosmetic uses of seaweed are numerous and it is used as an active dispersing and thickening agent in creams, lotions, gels, powders, soaps, and shampoos.

"Even households generate hazardous waste from items such as cleaning detergents and scouring pads necessary for cleaning. Often, this waste is hazardous and dangerous to both nature and human life. The levels of dangerous wastes continue to grow."

Namita Rautray, Eco-Manufacturer
Inovex Enterprises PVT. LTD. | inovexenterprises.com

# Guide to Green Fabrics

Eco-friendly textiles for fashion and interior design

guidetogreenfabrics.com

Sea Grass

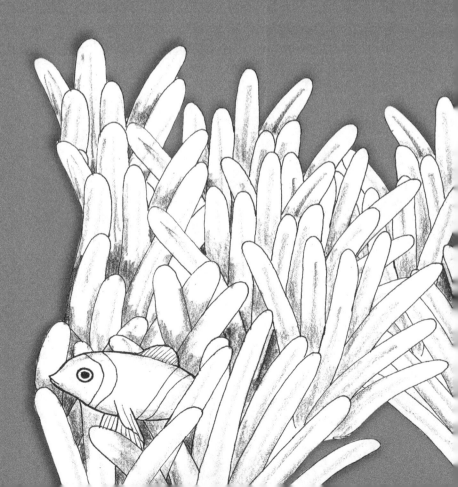

Long, narrow, leafy marine flowering plants that grow in meadows like formations in the sea are labeled "sea grass" and the fibers derived from these are used to create some of the finest and most stylish home accessories in the world. It is a wholly organic, biodegradable, naturally occurring resource, which can be used for a variety of purposes, especially in the home furnishings sector.

Sea grass is primarily grown in South East Asian nations with China, Vietnam, and India leading the supply of fibers. It is grown in paddy fields, which are flooded with sea water.

Sea grass is a wonderful friend of the environment as it engineers the creation of its own habitat in the seas. Its leaves control the flow of sediments that travel through the rivers, and its own roots and rhizomes hold the seabed together. Creating a natural impediment to the harmful effects of fast moving sea currents, sea grass is also an important shelter for several small plant and animal species. As such, this aids in the protection of the eco-system.

Harvested sea grass is dried naturally in the sun after which it is spun into an exceptionally strong fiber, which is highly resistant to wear and tear. The fiber is also allowed to retain certain impurities, and these impart each product with a unique look. Sea grass is one of the most environmentally friendly of all organic materials because it is generally allowed to retain its natural green color, thus doing away with the dyeing process altogether.

Sea grass rugs, the most common use for these fibers as an eco-friendly interior accessory, are used as carpeting in offices and places where there is a large amount of human traffic. Cleaning the fiber is relatively easy since dirt does not readily adhere to it, and the natural color of the fiber conceals dirt. Spills and stains are easy to contain due to the low absorbency and hard nature of the fiber. Sea grass has very good anti-static, anti-burn, and anti-stain properties. Not only this, it absorbs noise and is a good thermal insulator.

Sea grass is a completely green fiber as there are no chemical inputs in growing, harvesting, and fabricating the fiber, and also because it is 100% biodegradable. It holds much promise to be one of the most important fibers of the future.

"Peace silk, also known as ahimsa silk, is my favorite fabric. Although
I don't use it in my collections I have friends that are designers who use
this fabric and it's absolutely incredible."

Beth Doane, Green Fashion Designer
RainTees | raintees.com

# Guide to Green Fabrics

## Eco-friendly textiles for fashion and interior design

guidetogreenfabrics.com

Silk

## Overview

The story of silk dates back to pre-historic times, but the earliest records of silk have been traced to about 2600 B.C. when the Empress Si-Ling, also called the "Goddess of the Silkworm," raised silkworms explicitly for making fibers from their cocoons. Another version of the origin of silk is traced to yet another Chinese princess who was said to be sipping tea in her garden when a cocoon, dangling from a branch, fell into her hot tea. It suddenly released threads of silk, which later became the chosen fiber of the Imperial household. Today, there are a variety of silk harvesting and production methods, and in seeking green alternatives, a new crop of sustainable and responsibly produced silks have emerged. The consumer must wade through the facts and integrate their priorities and preferences into selection of the kinds of silk they feel best meet their environmental missions. While all of the finished silks offer time-less luster and luxury appeal, some are greener than others. As new production methods come to light, a fair assessment is that the green community will purposefully exercise choice in the matters of silk.

From a historical perspective, China's mastery of silk production made the fiber an important component of its economy in ancient times. The trade of silk with Europe and the Near East led to the establishment of the fabled "Silk Route," used chiefly for trading in silk. Aristotle, Alexander, the ancient Greeks and Romans, the fathers of the early church, and European nobility soon became admirers of this lustrous, free draping fabric leading to the universalization of silk fabric. The Chinese zealously guarded the art of making silk, but like all coveted arts this too was smuggled out of the country to nearby Japan in 300 A.D. from where it slowly made its way to India, Spain, and Italy. Although the silk industry has spread to many parts of the world, the finest silks are still being produced by China, Japan, India, Spain, Italy, and France.

## Properties

In any case presented, the finished fibers are clearly considered some of the most lustrous and luxurious in the world. The silkworm's method of extruding protein and spinning it into silk is unmatched. This results in fibers that are super strong, but not very elastic. Silk has good moisture regain, but loses one fifth of its strength when wet. Direct sunlight weakens and damages silk so care must be taken to shield it. It is susceptible to attack by insects, therefore, proper storage is essential. Silk is a poor conductor of electricity and will produce static cling, but softeners may be used to control this. The luxury nature of silk makes it quite sought after, as it is smooth and fluid to the touch. It is hypoallergenic in nature with outstanding drape qualities. Silk is breathable and very insulating. A durable and resilient fabric, it is also abrasion resistant and versatile. Luckily, wearers stay cool in summer and warm in winter due to its natural insulating properties.

## Production/ Environmental Concerns

Traditional silk is made from the cocoons of silkworms (moth caterpillars, *Bombyx mori*), which feed on an exclusive diet of mulberry leaves. Silk production is carried out in a controlled environment and this is known as *sericulture*. Healthy eggs are reared up to the *chrysalis* (pupa) stage and when the chrysalis has made the cocoon around itself, just before it can break out of it, the silk fiber is extracted. The chrysalis are destroyed in a process called *storing*, which means stifling them with the application of heat.

Each cocoon produces silk thread between 1,000 to 2,000 feet in length. *Fibroin*, which is the fiber, constitutes about 75-90% of the cocoon while the other 10% is made up of *sericin*, or the gum that holds the fibers together in the form of the cocoon. The cocoons are taken to the filature after being stored, where they are sorted according to color and size, so as to yield silk fiber of uniform quality. The sericin is released from the cocoon to facilitate removal of fiber after it has been brushed to reveal the end of the fiber. The fiber is then threaded through an eyelet made of porcelain and it is reeled onto a wheel continuously using scores of cocoons. The fibers are bound together naturally during spinning due to certain amounts of sericin, which are deliberately retained during the washing process. From these reels, skeins of silk are made. The remaining sericin is washed off by soaking them in warm water mixed with oil or soap. This process brings down the weight of the fiber by almost 25%. The degummed fibers are then ready to be dyed into various colors, and prepared for weaving or knitting. The texture of silk fabric is achieved during the yarn twisting process, and tight twisting of fibers gives sheer fabric while loose twisting gives thick fabric, when woven or knitted.

The shimmer, or luster, of silk is the single most characteristic that has captivated people from time immemorial and this is due to its structure. The fiber has a triangular, almost prismatic, structure that causes refraction of light at various angles leading to the diffusion of a variety of shades from the fabric. Numerous synthetics have tried to imitate silk's luster, but it is never good enough and doesn't capture the spectacular, rich beauty offered by this special fiber.

Beyond this, there is a single step in the above process that ignites the conversation about silk and how green and humane it is across the board. Although silk is a sustainable fiber, animal treatment becomes a factor due to the heat application that kills the moths before they can emerge from the cocoon. This is done with traditional silk production in an effort to preserve the filament quality of the fiber and not break it, degrading its marketability. Accordingly, silk is the only naturally long filament yarn in the world, as all other natural fibers are of short, *staple* length. Silkworms may also be injected with hormone disrupters that control growth rate, lengthening the time silkworms produce silk. Pesticides and insecticides have routinely been used in traditional silk production as well. There are pros and cons in determining the use of all of the types of available silk, and the more detail given to the end user the better for their own education in design planning and execution.

Alternately, *ahimsa silk*, also known as peace silk, offers two varieties: cultivated and wild. Peace silk simply provides more options based upon green ideologies and individual choice. An organic (peace silk) alternative, called organic silk or raw silk, challenges traditional cultivation and production methods by offering eco-focused harvesting, and does not infuse pesticides, insecticides, or chemical treatments into the process. Although these silkworms are often farmed, the employed techniques are sustainable and natural. Mulberry trees continue to be the source of food for silkworms that produce organic silk, which is 100% biodegradable. With organic silk, silkworms are given ethical treatment and allowed to live their full lives while dying naturally, about five days after laying their eggs. A factor here is that there are several hundred eggs that all require immediate care and feeding, and to care for all of them is often impossible, therefore most of them perish naturally.

In traditional silk cultivation, only one pupa is killed prior to hatching. Although not ethical in many eyes, the alternative is that hundreds of would-be pupa will not survive in raw silk cultivation, but it is greener due to the lack of chemical infusion. However, the silk produced is of a lower quality and not as smooth as traditional silk.

silk dupioni fabric

Silk is a poor conductor of electricity and will produce static cling,
but softeners may be used to control this. The luxury nature of silk
makes it quite sought after, as it is smooth and fluid to the touch.
It is hypoallergenic in nature with outstanding drape qualities.

Wild silk, or Tussah silk (China) or Tasar silk (India), is associated with a more natural way of raising silkworms, such as in natural tree environments with natural movement and eating patterns. These silkworms do not live on mulberry trees exclusively, but roam naturally amongst a variety of trees. Considering that naturally hatched cocoons (where the moth emerges on its own) produce staple fibers in general (because of tearing), it is common practice that wild silk cocoons are plucked from the natural trees. They are then opened to expose the pupa, and it too is normally destroyed by heat or hot water. These cocoons provide reeled silk, or long filament yarns, which are higher in quality and price. In countries like China and India pupa are also used as food, and in China, for traditional medicine. Hence, there is a secondary market for pupa, but there are also those cocoons that are left to mature naturally. However, it is a small percentage overall. As evidenced, there are pros and cons to consider with all methods, and it's the consumer's responsibility to explore the greenest options for their own clarity and comfort.

## Color/Dyeability

A protein fiber, silk is best dyed using the acid dye method, where the dye is incorporated into the fiber at a cellular level. Natural dyes may be used in coloring raw silk to beautiful tones, and there are also natural colors from golden to reddish-brown. Traditional silk has been dyed in every imaginable hue with spectacular results.

## End Uses

Silk has long been sought after for the production of myriad consumer products of the highest quality. When one hears "silk," the automatic response is that the associated product has a higher standard and will be of more value simply due to the fiber therein. Silk is used worldwide for men's and women's garments, children's clothes, jackets, scarves, sweaters, hats, and all types of accessories. In household furnishings it is used to make pillows, luxury throws, and cushion covers, among other luxury items. Printed or painted, silk may even be framed as art.

## Care

Because of its value, silk calls for a certain amount of hand care while washing and storing. It should be washed using a mild soap and alkaline-based detergents are best avoided as this may weaken the fabric, as does soaking it for a long time or using bleach. After washing and rinsing the garment in cold water, it should be allowed to drip dry or be pressed between towels to remove water. Silk tends to be weak when wet, so at this stage it must be handled carefully. Adding a capful of vinegar or lemon juice to the final rinse restores the luster that is lost during the washing process. Light ironing from the inside out is recommended. If followed properly, these tips lead to good care and ensure that the garment performs beautifully over time.

## Silk

100% biodegradable (organic silk)
Has high breathability qualities
Colorfast, offering lovely, bright colors
Outstanding drape qualities
Lacks elasticity
Poor conductor of electricity
Hypoallergenic
Susceptible to attack by insects
Very insulating, keeps you warm and cool
Extremely lustrous, highly sought after fabric
Good moisture regain
Smooth and fluid to the touch
Super strong and durable
Weakened by direct sunlight
Loses strength when wet

## Characteristics

# Guide to Green Fabrics™

### Eco-friendly textiles for fashion and interior design

guidetogreenfabrics.com

## Soybean Protein

## Overview

A uniquely advanced fiber now being used to make fabric comes from one of the greenest products found on our planet: soybean. Surely, it is one of the most abundantly produced agricultural goods whose cultivation and processing have minimum impact on the environment. Soybean Protein Fiber (SPF) has 16 amino acids that promote healthy skin invisibly while nourishing damaged skin. For the fashion conscious its appeal lies in its excellent drape and the smooth touch and feel of the fabric. It is also noted for the comfortable feeling it brings to the wearer. Its skin-friendly attributes are also espoused due to its anti-bacterial, anti-microbial, UV resistant, and hygroscopic qualities. Soybean is the only botanic protein fiber in the world, often referred to as "vegetable cashmere" for its smooth, soft appeal. It has become a favorite of manufacturers and designers who are on the lookout for fabrics that promote the health of the individual and the environment, requirements that soybean fibers meet totally.

Although only recently heralded for its green qualities on a more global scale, soybean protein is not a new fiber. The 1930's saw Henry Ford wearing soybean suits and using the fiber to make seat covers for his automobiles. His interest in developing soybean-based fuel was legendary. Soybean protein fiber is cultivated in almost all parts of the globe, although it was traditionally an East Asian crop grown in China, Japan, and Korea.

## Properties

Soybean fibers have a combination of the best qualities of natural and synthetic fibers. Due to a natural material being the main ingredient of the fiber, it retains the elegant luster and comfort of natural fabrics. Because it's produced in association with chemical additives, it takes on some of the qualities apparent in man-made fibers. As such, it has good tensile strength with no shrinkage, even in boiling water, and is easy to care for like most synthetic fabrics. Boasting excellent absorption qualities, soybean protein offers predictable dryness to wearers during hot weather.

Soybean protein can be blended with other fibers to showcase a multitude of new fabrics that combine the innate qualities of both. Pure soybean fabric has a distinct ivory color and the fabric has enormous fluff. When blended with cashmere the fabric gives a smooth feeling when worn and also nourishes the skin on account of its protein make-up. In conjunction with mercerized wool, it offers a superior fabric free from shrinkage, while cotton blended with soybean feels softer, and moisture absorption is enhanced along with better ventilation. Silk and soybean combine together to form an exquisite fabric that glows with a subtle luster and drapes and falls elegantly. As a bonus, it neutralizes the negative qualities of silk such as staining when wet and sticking to the body. With synthetic fiber blends, the fabric becomes extremely strong, durable, and free from creasing and wrinkles.

## Production

Soybean protein is the result of application of bioengineering advances in agriculture production. Because soybean has a different physical and chemical composition than other protein fibers, it must be handled with extreme care. The production process begins after tofu and soy milk have been extracted from the soybean. The leftover cake is distilled in order to realize the spherical protein.

soy and silk fashion scarf

Model: Tracie Stafford

Next, the protein is converted to liquid through a special process. Under the functioning of an auxiliary agent and biological enzyme, spherical protein's space structure changes and it liquefies. High polymers are added to this mixture and it is cooked. The protein is then passed through a spinneret that looks very much like a showerhead in a process called *wet-spinning*. The fibers are then stabilized by *acetalizing*. This liquid is solidified into protein fibers using multiple processes like chemical cross-linking, curving, thermal setting, and cutting. The finished fibers can be created in a variety of lengths. To prepare the actual yarns for fabric, scouring and bleaching the fibers during the pretreatment process removes the oils, lubricants, and pigments from the fiber, and this must be handled delicately. *Desizing* is done either by using enzymes, alkali, or oxidants. It must be remembered that soybean fibers cannot be mercerized because the fiber does not tolerate strong caustic soda.

## Environmental Concerns

Soybean protein is a green fiber with minimal impact on the environment, but the thoughtless cultivation of this plant in Brazil and Argentina, especially, raises the hackles of the green community. Large tracts of rain forests, which are the lungs of the earth, are cleared away to cultivate this profitable crop, which has brought prosperity to the native population. Soybeans are also used in crop rotation as the product enriches the nitrogen content of soil. In order to give this fabric a greener label, these arbitrary methods of obtaining land and producing soybean need to be curtailed.

In other territories, responsible tracts of soybeans are cultivated in massive quantities, causing an inexpensive crop to be managed locally and exported globally. It is generally harvested without harmful chemicals, and the residue is often used as feed. Because the fabric is a by-product of soybean, it in fact uses up the soy cake and oil, and as such, helps the environment through utilization of discarded waste. Its biodegradability is yet another factor which works in its green favor.

## Color/Dyeability

Strong-willed in terms of its hue, soybean has a natural color called *curcuma*. It is a heavy pigment not easy to remove. The preferred method of removing this is by bleaching. Hydrogen peroxide or reduction bleaching methods can be used for this purpose. Should a whitening agent be used, it is important to note that the fabric will never be fully white, but faintly yellow in result. The process of dyeing comes after the fibers have been pretreated. These fibers take to dyeing fairly well and a variety of products can be used to add color including reactive and non-reactive dyes. The dyeing fastness of soybean fibers is similar to wool.

## End Uses

The softness and suppleness of the fabric make it ideal for creating undergarments. Its anti-microbial, anti-bacterial quality makes it the ideal fabric for use in baby clothes and nightwear, as well as other items for the needs of people with allergies. Its use in making body fitting undergarments is unmatched as it does not irritate the skin in spite of being closely fitted. Soybean protein is used to make lovely clothing items such as shirts, tops, sweaters, and jackets. Its appeal as a bed linen is also matchless due to its softness and health benefits.

## Care

Soybean protein fabric can be machine washed on the gentle cycle with mild detergent or hand washed, but strictly without bleach during either method. It can withstand air drying or a light dryer cycle without fabric softener. Items can be laid flat to dry naturally and will remain soft. Because the fabric is soft and pliable and has good elasticity, ironing may not be necessary for certain garments. However, if ironing is desired, a low setting is preferred.

## Soybean Protein

Has 16 amino acids that promote healthy skin
Anti-bacterial
Anti-microbial
UV resistant
100% biodegradable
Only botanic protein fiber in the world
Offers a distinct, golden ivory color
Has good dyeing properties, colorfast
Extremely comfortable
Has excellent drape and smooth touch
Considered an easy care fabric
Enriches the nitrogen content of soil
Minimal environmental impact
Has good hygroscopic qualities
Lightweight, dries quickly and easily
Elegantly lustrous, luxurious appeal
Soft and supple, has cashmere-like qualities
Has high tensile strength with no shrinkage
Has better ventilation than cotton
Warmth retention similar to wool

## Characteristics

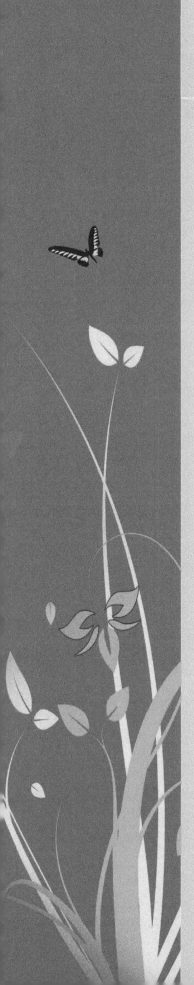

# Designer Spotlight

## Beth Doane

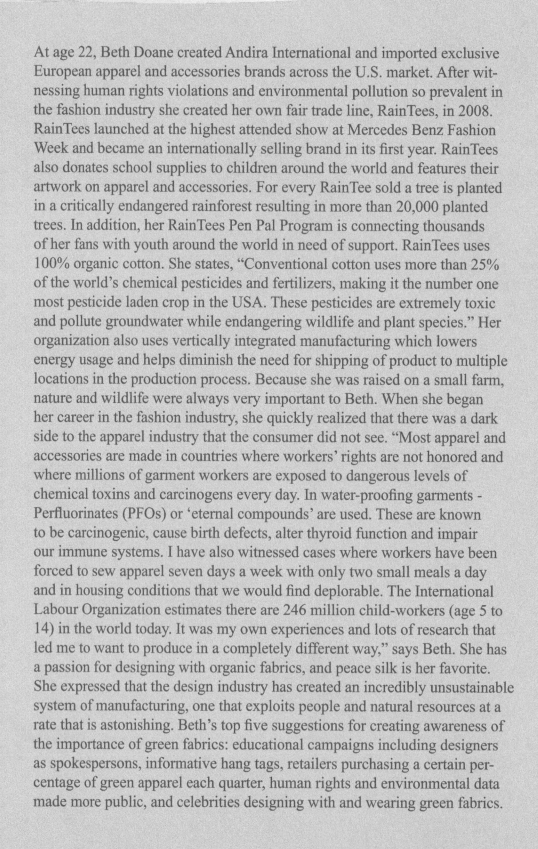

At age 22, Beth Doane created Andira International and imported exclusive European apparel and accessories brands across the U.S. market. After witnessing human rights violations and environmental pollution so prevalent in the fashion industry she created her own fair trade line, RainTees, in 2008. RainTees launched at the highest attended show at Mercedes Benz Fashion Week and became an internationally selling brand in its first year. RainTees also donates school supplies to children around the world and features their artwork on apparel and accessories. For every RainTee sold a tree is planted in a critically endangered rainforest resulting in more than 20,000 planted trees. In addition, her RainTees Pen Pal Program is connecting thousands of her fans with youth around the world in need of support. RainTees uses 100% organic cotton. She states, "Conventional cotton uses more than 25% of the world's chemical pesticides and fertilizers, making it the number one most pesticide laden crop in the USA. These pesticides are extremely toxic and pollute groundwater while endangering wildlife and plant species." Her organization also uses vertically integrated manufacturing which lowers energy usage and helps diminish the need for shipping of product to multiple locations in the production process. Because she was raised on a small farm, nature and wildlife were always very important to Beth. When she began her career in the fashion industry, she quickly realized that there was a dark side to the apparel industry that the consumer did not see. "Most apparel and accessories are made in countries where workers' rights are not honored and where millions of garment workers are exposed to dangerous levels of chemical toxins and carcinogens every day. In water-proofing garments - Perfluorinates (PFOs) or 'eternal compounds' are used. These are known to be carcinogenic, cause birth defects, alter thyroid function and impair our immune systems. I have also witnessed cases where workers have been forced to sew apparel seven days a week with only two small meals a day and in housing conditions that we would find deplorable. The International Labour Organization estimates there are 246 million child-workers (age 5 to 14) in the world today. It was my own experiences and lots of research that led me to want to produce in a completely different way," says Beth. She has a passion for designing with organic fabrics, and peace silk is her favorite. She expressed that the design industry has created an incredibly unsustainable system of manufacturing, one that exploits people and natural resources at a rate that is astonishing. Beth's top five suggestions for creating awareness of the importance of green fabrics: educational campaigns including designers as spokespersons, informative hang tags, retailers purchasing a certain percentage of green apparel each quarter, human rights and environmental data made more public, and celebrities designing with and wearing green fabrics.

RainTees | raintees.com

Spider silk is a very strong fiber and it is estimated that a thin rope of spider silk measuring in thickness to a pencil can stop a Boeing 747 in motion. This equates the strength of spider silk to steel, although it offers only one-fifth its density.

# Guide to Green Fabrics™

Eco-friendly textiles for fashion and interior design

guidetogreenfabrics.com

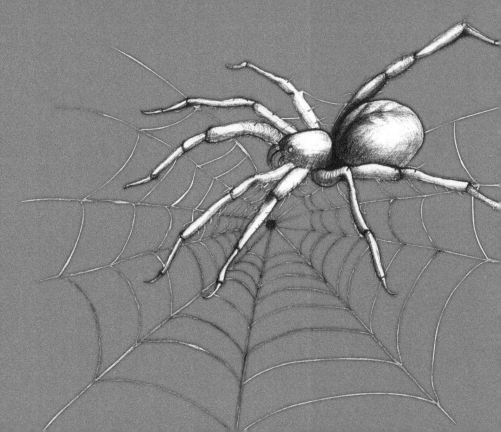

Spider Silk

## Overview

The thread of a spider's web, the spinning techniques employed by the spider, and the beautiful symmetry of the end product have fascinated all human beings who have set eyes upon it. The threads of the web are called spider silk, or *gossamer*, which is a kind of protein fiber spun by spiders, exhibiting extremely high tensile strength as well as flexibility. Humans have used spider silk for thousands of years, and the limited availability combined with its extraordinary applications has earned it the nickname "holy grail of fibers." In ancient times, it was valued more for its healing properties than as a clothing fiber.

A French missionary, Jacob Paul Cambone, living in Madagascar in the 1880's, took to the task of producing silk from spiders and engineered a machine that would employ 24 spiders at a single time. The chief goal was to collect their protein rich silk for commercial purposes. The process was designed to prevent harm to the spiders. In the end, although he managed to make a good amount of silk thread it was still not a commercially viable enterprise, and even today it is not.

## Properties

Spider silk is a very strong fiber and it is estimated that a thin rope of spider silk measuring in thickness to a pencil can stop a Boeing 747 in motion. This equates the strength of spider silk to steel, although it offers only one-fifth its density. Certain substances like pyrrolidine make the fiber hygroscopic and moist, while the acidic nature of the fiber keeps it safe from bacterial and fungal attacks. Compared to the silk spun by silkworms, spider silk is 10 times thinner but many times stronger. Its elasticity is double that of nylon while it is more difficult to break than even rubber. Spider silk can stretch up to 30 times its original length without breaking. With all these desirable qualities, it is a much sought after fiber, but the inability to produce it artificially has been the bane of scientists everywhere. To this day, this fiber's appeal as a super-fiber with unusual strength capacity, durability, and elasticity continues to inject mystery into the minds of scientists all over the world.

Researchers have tried to inject the spider silk gene into animals like cows and goats, and the milk of transgenic goats did produce the spider silk protein, but the resultant fiber did not quite match the qualities of the original. More specifically, in 2002, a Canadian-based company, Nexia Biotechnologies, Inc.™, was successful in developing the world's first spider silk fibers from man-made materials with properties similar to natural spider silk. This was accomplished via spider gene injection into goats, whose milk carried the gene throughout a proprietary transgenic goat technology process to produce wet-spun fibers trademarked BioSteel®. The goal was to produce BioSteel® in commercial quantities for multiple applications such as medical sutures, biodegradable fishing lines, soft body armor, and unique material composites. Development continues to be in progress.

## Production

Spider silk is difficult to replicate in the laboratory since it is created using a liquid protein, secreted by a special gland in the spider's belly. The spider, then using its spinnerets (usually seen in pairs, ranging from two to eight, depending on the species), and by application of physical force, re-arranges the molecular structure of the protein and turns it into a solid thread. It has such immense strength, flexibility, and tensile structure that it has baffled humans from decade to decade.

The main reason why man has not very successfully fabricated spider silk is because the spider's spinneret is what contributes to the strength of the protein fiber produced. It is the spider's certain concentration of material, PH, and pressure, which when squeezed out gives the fiber amazing qualities of strength. This derives from the specific arrangement of amino acids that form crystals and certain other amorphous domains. It is the symphony between these alternating structures that invests the fiber with its tenacious qualities.

## Environmental Concerns

Spider silk's eco-friendly character comes from the fact that it is made by animals without any chemical additives, and as such, there is no visible, adverse environmental impact. Spider silk is also 100% biodegradable.

## End Uses

Curiosity about spider silk's potential applications has spanned the ages. Early, resourceful pioneers often found enough of it to fashion important and beneficial items. Ancient Greeks used spider silk to make bandages to stop bleeding and also made use of its antiseptic properties. Gossamer was, and still is, used as crosshairs on telescopes, microscopes, and guns, and other such optical instruments. In Australia, Aborigines caught small fish with nets made of spider silk. Unfortunately, spider silk cloth production has not been realized except for on an extremely small scale, with reports of only a single 11' x 4' piece being produced in Madagascar by over eighty, diligent, spider-collecting creatives. Beyond this, Simon Peers and Nicholas Godley undertook a three-year, complex task of creating an embroidered piece of golden spider silk, and also designed a brocaded shawl made from the silk of more than one million female golden orb-weaver spiders collected in the highlands of Madagascar. Their cape, a glowing, glamorous, and spectacular design, went on display for the first time from January to June 2012 at the Victoria and Albert Museum in London.

Interestingly, the ferocious and territorial nature of the spider protects the species from over-hunting, thus leading to its safety. However, these circumstances also lead to death of the spiders. The course of nature proves that the territorial nature of the spiders causes them to kill each other on occasions of close proximity, and this limits production even further. Spiders may also be isolated and simply perish. Sorrowfully, this exhibits the reality of extreme limited production of this precious silk. Because spider silk is so fine, it would take over 400 spiders just to make one square yard of cloth. Therefore, large-scale spider silk clothing production is yet a dreamy fantasy due to these conditions.

## Spider Silk

Anti-bacterial
Anti-fungal
Has anti-septic properties
100% biodegradable
No chemical additives
Unusually flexible and elastic
Hygroscopic and moist
Estimated to be as strong as steel
with only one-fifth density
Has extremely high tensile strength
10 times thinner than silk from
silkworms, yet much stronger

## Characteristics

"Individuals often throw out goods without realizing that they are headed for a landfill and could be dangerous for the environment. No matter where people put these hazardous waste materials, there is always a chance that they could find their way into the ground and eventually into our bodies."

Namita Rautray, Eco-Manufacturer
Inovex Enterprises PVT. LTD. | inovexenterprises.com

# Guide to Green Fabrics™

## Eco-friendly textiles for fashion and interior design

guidetogreenfabrics.com

Tencel® / Lyocell

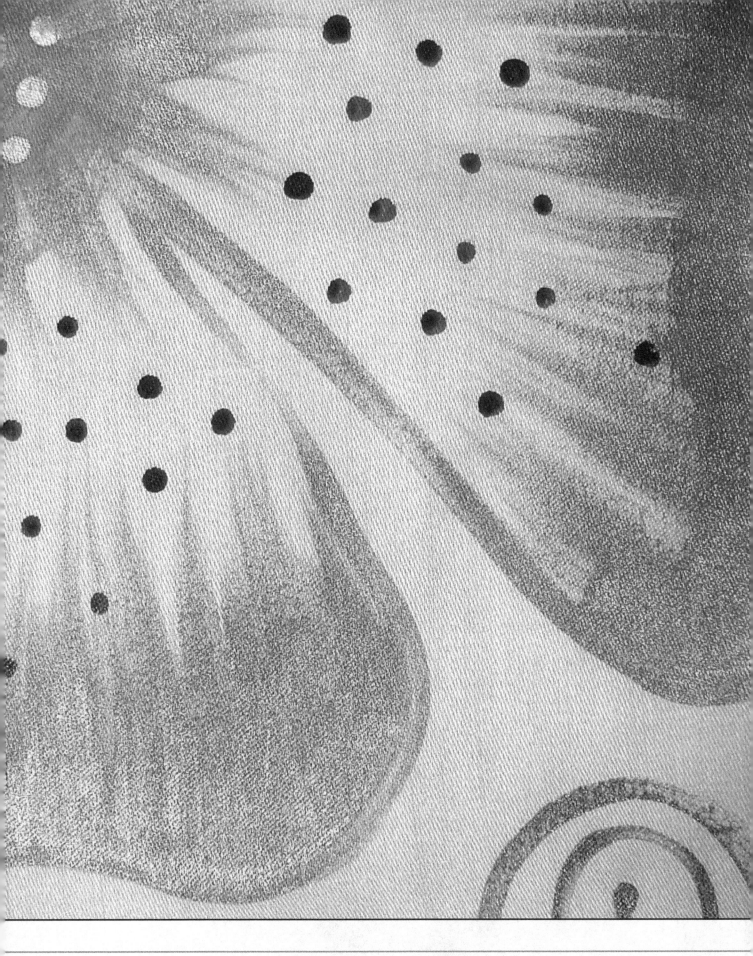

Hand painted details on bamboo rayon napkins by Kristene Smith

Tencel® was first made by Courtaulds Fibers UK™ in 1987, but at present only Lenzing Fibers, Inc.™ in the United States is its known manufacturer. Tencel® is the trade name for lyocell, a man-made natural fiber. It has an extremely flattering drape that clings sensuously to the human form, sending out a signal of luxurious elegance. It is soft, breathable, lightweight, comfortable, and shrink resistant. It has good strength not only when wet, but also when dry. It dyes uniformly and all colors have the propensity to acquire a richer look when applied to this fabric.

Tencel® is routinely blended with other fibers such as silk, cotton, rayon, polyester, wool, and linen. It has a supple quality when it is blended with cotton, and with synthetic fibers it adds a dimension of shape retention to the fabric. The fiber is considered a sub-species of rayon.

Lyocell is made from wood pulp cellulose using the solvent spinning process. The fiber is created after the wood pulp has been dissolved in N-Methylmorpholine N-Oxide leading to the creation of a new solution called *dope*. This dope is passed through a spinneret to create lyocell fibers which are further washed to remove chemicals. The water containing the chemicals is purified and re-used, which allows this fiber to be known as one of the most eco-conscious in the world because of its recycling-centered production methods. Generally, chemicals used in processing are non-toxic and 99% recyclable. However, additional chemical treatments that assist lyocell in accepting color and dyes may be harsher, so this needs to be considered when choosing green fabrics for design purposes.

Staple fibers (short fibers) are used in making denim, chino undergarments, and other such apparel, while filament fibers (long fibers) are used to make high end men's and women's apparel since these fibers have a silky appearance. Tencel® has the quality of fibrillation whereby the wet fabric, after undergoing abrasion, exhibits micro fibrils on its surface. These micro-fibrils can be manipulated in such a way that they give the fabric distinct variety in appearance, like a peach skin surface.

Garments made of Tencel® do not need extraordinary care, but it is advisable to hand wash and drip dry them. Ironing the garments using a warm iron is the best way to remove wrinkles.

As noted in other chapters, consumer knowledge of fiber procurement, harvesting, and production methods is key to determining a green fabric. Natural plant-based fibers that endure chemical intensity may not be the most eco-conscious fibers available, so their comparison is necessary when considering options. Other factors, such as water purification and dyeing methods, also play a role in the fabric decision making process.

"Educating people is the first step in creating awareness of green fabrics. A majority of people are unaware of how easy using green fabrics can be. Explaining the benefits of green fabrics and the positive impact it will have on them and the environment is vital."

Sarah Barnard, Green Interior Designer
Sarah Barnard Design | sarahbarnarddesign.blogspot.com

# Guide to Green Fabrics™

Eco-friendly textiles for fashion and interior design

guidetogreenfabrics.com

Wild Nettle

When wild nettle, a weed that grows rampant in remote villages in the Himalayan nation of Nepal, began to be seen as an exciting new fiber, the livelihood of the people living there saw drastic, positive improvement. In fact, the stinging nettle, which scares away most people, is now being turned into designer wear by several international fashion houses, and its eco-friendly method of cultivation and production gladdens the hearts of all designers with a clean, green conscience. The use of nettle for clothing is not a new concept, it's just that its benefits and utility have been re-discovered. Primitive man had always been innovative and his raiment was made from nettle, especially those living in areas where it grew abundantly. As a testament, and much to their credit, natives of the Algonquin tribe were known to make fishing nets from this fiber. Also, during the World Wars in the absence of adequate stocks of cotton, the German army turned towards making uniforms for their soldiers with fabric made from wild nettle.

It is found in almost all parts of the globe that enjoy a temperate climate. Being a weed, it spreads quickly without excess human input, and any soil that has been properly tended is the perfect breeding ground for this plant.

The fiber is extracted from its long stem. Nettle fibers are hollow on the inside and allow for accumulation of air, which creates a feeling of natural warmth. The same fiber can be used to make summer garments that have a cooling effect by twisting the fibers closely so that the hollowness is closed, and that prevents air from getting trapped inside.

The bark of the plant, from which the fiber is extracted, is collected manually and left in the sun to allow it to dry completely. After the fiber dries, it is once again put in water and soaked completely for more than a week. One of the steps involved with extracting fiber from the bark uses a mixture of ash and mountain spring water to which the bark is added and cooked for some time until almost all the water has evaporated. The bark is then washed well to rid it of the ash, after which it is beaten in order to release the fibers. The beaten bark and fibers are then dried.

Wild nettle is a fiber derived from a plant that sprouts by itself and it does no harm to the environment. Like some other natural fibers, the production methods are still manual requiring little chemical and technological input, leading to the introduction of a fiber that is totally green.

# Guide to Green Fabrics ™

Eco-friendly textiles for fashion and interior design

Exploring the true, scientific dynamics of textiles is an amazing study. It's like one of those sci-fi movies that shows the camera going underneath someone's skin and muscles to reveal the inner goings-on of the human body. Understanding fiber all the way down to the DNA is quite the same!

Knowing this, there is one fact not to be missed: that fabric begins with fibers and fabric is vital to the fashion and interior design industries, and others. When drilling down, it reveals *needing* to know what the fiber is about, what its origins are, what it can do, and how it will perform in a finished design. These are all vital questions needing answers. Therefore, the only genuine encouragement to offer revolves around seeing the fiber as your friend and really getting to know it and its myriad characteristics.

Emotionally speaking, fibers can take us in many directions. For example, remember the design that was supposed to flow like the wind, but instead was stiff as a board because polished cotton was substituted for silk? A quick nap in Textiles 101 never hurt anyone, right? What about the 'luster' that eluded the designer and instead was replaced with 'shine' in the final design? Or, your client wants an organic cotton summer dress and needs you to articulate the benefits of it over traditional cotton. Can you? You get the picture. And with that, you are the one who must package all of this knowledge as evidence of your genuine interest in your new best friends – the fibers!

For added encouragement, times have changed. We are now living in an eco-conscious, green-centric society and the backward button is perpetually broken. In fact, it never existed. This is a good thing. Demands are high and consumers are holding the bill – the cash, that is. As designers, we will meet these demands or become yesterday's news. The more environmentally conscious consumers become, the more we need to learn new ways of procuring materials that meet their needs and expectations.

Guide to Green Fabrics™ provides an overview of innovation in eco-textiles and enlightenment into the fascinating methods and properties that make green fabrics special. They're new and exciting and a few of them are even getting a second go around. There are ancient fibers seeing new light, time tested, chemical-free harvesting methods resurfacing, and new technologies being employed.

The best part is that you bring the creative vision for the actual design application through your love of art, color, nature, and inspiration. There is no design without you. Accordingly, when you take time to think smarter going forward and align yourself with where business is headed, you take notice of all components of the process, not just the creative elements. As we move into new, green territory together, new vistas in design will emerge and you'll find yourself at the forefront of an amazing movement.

Here's hoping you'll be aboard that train!

Kristene Smith

Kristene Smith is the author of Guide to Green Fabrics™. Initially launched as an educational research project on bamboo, her discovery of the world's leading green fibers blossomed into an educational learing suite now available to designers, students, textiles professionals, consumers, libraries and universities across the globe.

Green Earth News blogger Stacey Irwin writes, "An informed consumer is a true friend of the environment. But with the amount of information floating around both on the internet and through word-of-mouth, those wanting to make smart choices can easily be overwhelmed and misled. _Thankfully, Kristene Smith's Guide to Green Fabrics™ is on the market to help! I personally appreciate that this is truly a book for everyone whether you're a member of a knitting circle or an aspiring fashion designer. We can all make a difference with our fabric selections."

With its depth and breadth of information, Guide to Green Fabrics™ has become the definitive resource on green fabric education. Kristene Smith holds great expectations for the inevitable impact of this eco-friendly fabric guide, stating, "The textiles and apparel industry, with its massive economic engine, touches every life. From clothes and bedding to car interiors and medical supplies, textiles are indeed woven into our collective fabric of life. Truly knowing what our fabric choices are can help us make greener buying decisions."

A consultant, author, and designer, Kristene Smith holds a degree in Family and Consumer Science and lives with her family in California.

**Acetalizing**, an organic reaction that involves the formation of an acetal or ketal (p. 154).

**Agave fourcroydes**, technical name for the agave plant, which produces henequen/ sisal (p. 55).

**Ahimsa silk**, also known as peace silk, which offers two varieties: cultivated and wild (p. 147).

**Alkaline bath**, a solution used in conjunction with bleaching fabric (p. 28).

**Antimony**, a toxic chemical compound that is similar to compounds found in arsenic, it is converted to antimony trioxide when it reaches high temperatures (p. 128).

**Bacteriostatic**, inhibits the growth or reproduction of bacteria (p. 76).

**Bamboo kun**, bio-agent found in bamboo which gives it anti-bacterial qualities (p. 15).

**Barong tagalong**, formal dresses and wedding dresses of the Philippines (p. 115).

**Biodegradable**, capable of being broken down (p. 32).

**Biodiversity**, an environment indicated by numbers of different species of plants and animals (p. 9, 97).

**Biopolymer**, a polymer produced by living organisms (p. 60).

**Biotechnology**, the manipulation of living organisms to produce useful commercial products (p. 60).

**Boehmeria nivea**, technical name for ramie (p. 118).

**Bombyx mori**, technical name for the moth caterpillar (p. 146).

**Bud grafting**, the process of ensuring genetically identical trees to produce a pure product (p. 84).

**Cambium,** a tissue layer that provides undifferentiated cells for plant growth (p. 84).

**Cannabis genus**, the family of plants from which hemp is cultivated (p. 46).

**Cannabis sativa**, technical name for true hemp (p. 8).

**Capra hircus langier**, scientific name for the cashmere goat (p. 88).

**Carbon dioxide**, a heavy, colorless gas ($CO_2$) that does not support combustion, dissolves in water to form carbonic acid, is formed especially in animal respiration and in the decay or combustion of animal and vegetable matter, is absorbed from the air by plants in photosynthesis, and is used in the carbonation of beverages (p. 65).

**Carbon emissions**, technically named Carbon Dioxide Emissions, these are produced naturally through the carbon cycle and through human activities like the burning of fossil fuels (p. 41).

**Carbon footprint**, the total set of greenhouse gas (GHG) emissions caused by an organization, event, product, or person (p. 41).

**Carbonization**, a chemical process used to remove impurities from raw animal fibers (p. 137).

**Carcinogens**, a substance or agent causing cancer (p. 128).

**Carding**, a process of opening and cleaning textile fibers, usually cotton, which separates fibers from each other, lays them parallel, forms them into a thin web, and then condenses them into a single continuous untwisted strand or bundle of fibers called a "sliver" (p. 47).

**Caustic solution**, a solution containing sodium hydroxide (p. 28).

**Cellulose**, the naturally occurring polymer that forms the solid framework of plants (p. 22).

**Centrifuging**, the use of centrifugal force to remove water from wet textiles (p. 85).

**Charka**, a spinning wheel used to make coir yarns (p. 23).

**Chrysalis**, the pupa state of butterflies (p. 146).

**Clean technology**, a means to create electricity and fuels with a smaller environmental footprint (p. 40).

**Climate change**, a long-term change in the statistical distribution of weather patterns over periods of time (p. 69).

**Closed-loop**, a manufacturing resource planning model that incorporates returned products as part of the supply chain (p. 42).

**Coco peat**, a coconut husk by-product containing millions of capillary micro-sponges that have an extremely high ability to absorb and retain water (p. 25).

**Cocos Nucifera L**, technical name for the coconut tree, a palm tree species (p. 22).

**Coir dust**, another term for coir pith, used as soil substitute, mulch, and conditioner (p. 25).

**Coir pith**, coconut's non-fibrous connective tissue (p. 22).

**Colorfast**, a term used to describe a dyed fabric's ability to resist fading due to washing, exposure to sunlight, and other environmental conditions (p. 33).

**Combing**, an additional step beyond carding whereby fibers are arranged in a highly parallel form, and additional short fibers are removed, producing high quality yarns with excellent strength, fineness, and uniformity (p. 89).

**Crimp**, the inherent and natural waviness of wool (p. 89, 108, 136).

**Curcuma**, the natural, deep ivory color of soybean fibers (p. 154).

**Decortication**, the process of removing the woody, pithy matter from bast fibers through mechanical means (p. 68).

**Defoliation**, the removal of leaves from the cotton plant (p. 97).

**Dehairing**, a process of separating coarse upper hair from the soft undercoat of the cashmere goat (p. 88).

**De-husking**, the process of driving a coconut through a spike secured to the ground and splitting it (p. 23).

**Desizing**, the process of removing sizing materials from yarns or fabric, usually by application of acid or enzymes (p. 154).

**Dewatering**, a process wherein the water content of milk is removed to get it ready for skimming (p. 76).

**Dope**, the solution of a fiber forming polymer, usually extruded through spinnerets (p. 166).

**Down**, soft hairs of the cashmere goat (p. 89).

**Ecosystem**, a biological environment consisting of all the organisms living in a particular area, as well as all the nonliving physical components of the environment with which the organisms interact, such as air, soil, water, and sunlight (p. 126).

**Environmentally-friendly**, a term used to refer to goods and services, laws, guidelines and policies claimed to inflict minimal or no harm on the environment (p. 14).

**Epicarp**, the smooth, waterproof outer skin of the coconut husk (p. 22).

**Ethylene glycol**, an organic compound widely used as an automotive antifreeze and a precursor to polymers (p. 28).

**Exocarp**, the husk of the coconut (p. 22).

**Fibroin**, a type of protein found in silk fiber (p. 147).

**Filament**, long, continuous fibers (p. 114).

**Flax**, the plant from which linen is derived, and another name for linen (p. 104).

**Geotextile**, textiles used in agricultural applications, such as farming or landscaping (p. 25).

**Gossamer**, technical name for spider silk (p. 160).

**Greased wool**, sheared wool that has not been scoured (p. 137).

**Growth marks**, the result of damage caused to cattle by barbed wire or horns of other cattle (p. 40).

**Hand**, the feel of a fiber against the skin, whether it is soft or rough (p. 136).

**Heckling comb**, a device used to remove the fibrous core and impurities from flax (p. 105).

**Hectare**, a unit of area defined as 10,000 square meters (p. 46).

**Hemicellulose**, any of several heteropolymers (matrix polysaccharides), such as arabinoxylans, present along with cellulose in almost all plant cell walls (p. 64).

**Herbicides**, a type of pesticide used to kill unwanted plants (p. 47).

**Hevea brasiliensis**, technical name for the rubber tree (p. 84).

**Hibiscus cannabinus**, technical name for the plant that produces kenaf (p. 68).

**Hydro-extractor**, a machine used to remove excess moisture from fibers (p. 25, 89).

**Hydrophobic**, a characteristic where the fiber's exterior repels water, therefore keeping one dry (p. 136).

**Hygroscopic**, a term meaning water absorbent (p. 80, 136).

**Inherent qualities**, qualities and characteristics naturally found in a plant or animal (p. 69).

**Kashmir**, an Indian state (p. 88).

**Lanolin**, a yellow waxy substance secreted by the sebaceous glands of wool-bearing animals (p. 137).

**Lignin**, a complex chemical compound most commonly derived from wood, and an integral part of the secondary cell walls of plants and some algae (p. 22).

**Luster**, the natural glow of a fabric; not artificially shiny (p. 136).

**Mercerization**, the process of treating a cotton yarn or fabric in which the fabric or yarn is immersed in a caustic soda solution and later neutralized in acid (p. 16).

**Mesocarp**, the fibrous zone of the coconut (p. 22).

**Methane gas**, a harmful by-product of decomposing waste found in dumps and landfills (p. 123).

**Modacrylic fiber**, the industry name for modal (p. 80).

**Moso bamboo**, an edible variety of bamboo (p. 14).

**Musa sapientum**, technical name for the banana plant (p. 8).

**Musa textilis**, technical name for abaca, belonging to the banana and plantain family (p. 8).

**Natural tanning**, methods that use organic materials, such as extracts from bark and vegetables, rather than traditional tanning chemicals (p. 41).

**Natural wax**, a naturally occurring substance found amongst natural fibers (p. 40).

**Needle-felting**, a process in which fibers are matted together (p. 26).

**Noil**, short wool fibers that remain after combing (p. 89).

**Organic**, a term used to denote products made without harmful substances or processing methods that pass strict industry regulations (p. 40).

**Owling**, a term used to describe the smuggling of wool (p. 136).

**Oxygen**, a reactive element that is found in water, in most rocks and minerals, in numerous organic compounds, and as a colorless, tasteless, odorless diatomic gas constituting 21% of the atmosphere (p. 65).

**Ozone layer**, an atmospheric layer that is normally characterized by high ozone content which blocks most solar ultraviolet radiation from entry into the lower atmosphere (p. 76).

**Pashm**, the Persian word for wool (p. 90).

**Pashmina**, the softest form of cashmere (p. 90).

**Patina**, a sheen produced by age, wear, and polishing, or any such acquired change of a surface through age and exposure (p. 40).

**Pectin**, any of various water-soluble substances that bind adjacent cell walls in plant tissues and yield a gel which is the basis of fruit jellies (p. 105).

**Petioles**, abaca's long, broad, overlapping leaf stalks (p. 9).

**Phloem**, the part of the jute plant that contains the useful fiber (p. 64).

**Pill**, small, sometimes round, accumulations of fibers found on a fabric's surface (p. 80).

**Piña**, the Spanish word for pineapple (p. 114).

**Poaceae**, true grass family from a group of perennial evergreens related to bamboo (p. 14).

**Polyethylene terephthalate (PET)**, technical name for traditional polyester (p. 32).

**Polymer**, a chemical compound or mixture of compounds formed by polymerization and consisting essentially of repeating structural units (p. 54).

**Post-consumer waste**, waste derived from consumers through recycling efforts (p. 122).

**Post-industrial waste**, waste derived from a manufacturing process (p. 122).

**Pre-consumer waste**, material discarded prior to consumer use (p. 122).

**Press cloth**, a cloth made of natural fibers used to keep an iron from directly impacting fabric (p. 90).

**Ratt**, a device used to spin coir fibers (p. 23).

**Reaper**, a machine used to cut standing grain (p. 54).

**Recycled**, utilization of a product at the end of its lifecycle for new products (p. 60).

**Refuse**, unwanted or useless material (p. 32).

**Renewable resource**, a natural resource replaced by natural processes and replenished over time (p. 60).

**Retting**, a time period during which a plant is soaked in fresh and/ or sea water (p. 23).

**Rippling**, a process to deseed linen (p. 105).

**Rubber**, the product that results in latex not being treated with ammonia (p. 84).

**Scouring**, the process of removing dirt, animal grease, sand, vegetable matter, and various impurities from certain fibers (p. 64, 89, 137).

**Scutching**, removal of the woody portion of the flax stem by crushing it between a set of rollers (p. 105).

**Sericin**, the gum that holds silk fibers together in the form of the cocoon (p. 147).

**Sericulture**, the controlled environment governing traditional silk production (p. 146).

**Shive**, the broken stalk of the flax plant (p. 105).

**Sinamay/Sinnamay**, consumer name for woven abaca (p. 8).

**Skimming**, that which is skimmed from a liquid (p. 76).

**Slubs**, a defect that appears as small knots found scattered throughout a fabric (p. 104).

**Smallholdings**, small, rubber tree groves (p. 84).

**Soil erosion**, the process of weathering and transport of solids in the natural environment (p. 55).

**Sorting**, the process of sorting fibers or hairs by grade and color (p. 89).

**Spinneret**, a showerhead-like nozzle used to extrude liquid solution to make fibers (p. 15).

**Spinning**, a process used to create yarns (p. 15, 89).

**Staple**, a term used to describe short fibers (p. 147).

**Staple length**, a specific length of wool fiber (p. 136).

**Storing**, a process by which chrysalis are destroyed by stifling them with heat application (p. 146).

**Sustainable**, whereby biological systems remain diverse, independent, and productive over time (p. 40).

**Tapping**, a bark slashing technique used to extract natural latex (p. 84).

**Tatami**, Japanese floor mats made from rush (p. 140).

**Thermal oxidation**, a process used to effectively destroy contaminants present in exhaust (p. 42).

**Thermo-mechanical pulping**, the process of using steam machines for fiber separation (p. 47).

**Thermostatic**, meaning fibers are warm in winter and cool in summer (p. 41).

**Top**, longer, parallel, wool fibers (p. 89).

**Tsootquij**, the Spanish given, Mayan appellation for henequen/ sisal (p. 54).

**Tuxies**, thin sheaths, made into strips, of abaca's outer stalks (p. 9).

**Vegetable tanning**, a tanning process using vegetable matter ingredients such as tree bark (p. 40).

**Wet milling**, the process of soaking extracted coir fibers in shallow pools of slow running (fresh) water to swell and soften them (p. 23).

**Wet spinning**, a process whereby a spinneret is submerged in a chemical bath that causes the fiber to precipitate, and then solidify, as it emerges (p. 154).

**Wicking**, the action of moisture not being absorbed by a fabric, but instead, evaporating upon its surface or being absorbed by another layer of fabric, thereby keeping it, and the wearer, dry (p. 60).

**Winnowing**, to expose fibers to a current of air so that waste matter is eliminated (p. 105).

**Wool classing**, the process of classifying wool into distinct categories (p. 109).

**Woolen yarn system**, a process of developing yarns of low bulk density that involves using staple fibers treated with oil (p. 89).

**Worsted yarn system**, a process of developing yarns using longer wool fibers that are more parallel; the main operations are carding, combing, drafting, and spinning (p. 89).

**Xylem**, the woody core of the jute plant (p. 64).

*Publisher's Note*: Many of the fibers/fabrics mentioned in these chapters are not available for retail due to a variety of circumstances including limited availability and proprietary concerns. We encourage those interested in procuring eco-fabrics to do independent research to find manufacturers and retailers who supply the public. Internet searches will provide a wide variety of sources that can be pursued. However, please be aware of yardage minimums when ordering as certain manufacturers only supply in large quantities. You will find a number of swatch kits available online as well. Realistically, you may also find yourself without resources to order a specific fiber, such as spider silk, because it is not commercially available at this time. However, local fabric stores and other online resources do carry many of the fabrics mentioned in this guide.

# Guide to Green Fabrics™

Eco-friendly textiles for fashion and interior design

Kristene Smith

# Guide to
## Green Fabrics™

Eco-friendly textiles for fashion and interior design